THE ROAD FROM AUTHORITARIANISM TO DEMOCRATIZATION IN INDONESIA

THE ROAD FROM AUTHORITARIANISM TO DEMOCRATIZATION IN INDONESIA

Paul J. Carnegie

THE ROAD FROM AUTHORITARIANISM TO DEMOCRATIZATION IN INDONESIA

Copyright © Paul J. Carnegie, 2010

All rights reserved.

Maps from the United States Central Intelligence Agency's World Factbook.

First published in 2010 by PALGRAVE MACMILLAN® in the United States – a division of St. Martin's Press LLC, 175 Fifth Avenue, New York, NY 10010.

Where this book is distributed in the UK, Europe and the rest of the world, this is by Palgrave Macmillan, a division of Macmillan Publishers Limited, registered in England, company number 785998, of Houndmills, Basingstoke, Hampshire RG21 6XS.

PALGRAVE MACMILLAN is the global academic imprint of the above companies and has companies and representatives throughout the world.

Palgrave® and Macmillan® are registered trademarks in the United States, the United Kingdom, Europe and other countries.

ISBN: 978–0–230–10242–2

Library of Congress Cataloging-in-Publication Data

Carnegie, Paul J.
    The road from authoritarianism to democratization in Indonesia / Paul J. Carnegie.
        p. cm.
    ISBN 978–0–230–10242–2 (alk. paper)
    1. Indonesia—Politics and government—1998–
2. Democratization—Indonesia. 3. Authoritarianism—Indonesia.
I. Title.
    JQ776.C37 2009
    320.9598—dc22

                                                    2009041615

A catalogue record of the book is available from the British Library.

Design by MPS Limited, A Macmillan Company

First edition: June 2010

10 9 8 7 6 5 4 3 2 1

Printed in the United States of America.

Indonesia has changed beyond recognition. It has a working parliament . . . a directly elected president, a free press, all kinds of NGOs and pressure groups, and a very active civil society. People who've been away from Indonesia and come back are amazed to see all of these things that just wouldn't have been conceivable even five years ago.

Edward McBride, *The Economist*, December 9, 2004

The new democracy is burdened, however, by a heavy legacy from Indonesian history, especially from Suharto's New Order, which lasted more than three decades. For the quality of post-Suharto democracy, the most critical of these legacies is a deeply-entrenched tradition of patrimonial politics, which is buttressed by the survival of powerful (political, bureaucratic, military and business) interests rooted in the country's New Order past . . . the outcome of the ongoing contest for power between these interests and the forces for deeper democratic reform will determine whether the patrimonial democracy that has developed . . . becomes a stable political order or evolves into a more liberal system.

Douglas Webber, Joint Sessions of the European Consortium
of Political Research, Granada, April 14–19, 2005

Dedicated to I, J, M, M

CONTENTS

PREFACE

The future stability and expansion of the democratic project has been a major issue in the international community since the end of the Cold War. Yet, the ambiguity of recent postauthoritarian settlements raises many a perplexing question about the process. This led me to consider how and why interpreting ambiguity matters in the study of democratization. In the following book, I want to suggest that the way we frame democratization is struggling to keep pace with changing realities. The implications of which are explored through mapping Indonesia's journey from authoritarianism. I hope this will generate discussion on its dynamics of change and debates about democratization more generally.

Acknowledgments

There are institutions and individuals that have made this book possible. I would like to acknowledge the School of Political Science and International Studies at the University of Queensland for giving me my initial opportunity to research Indonesian democratization. First, in particular, thanks go to Associate Professor David Martin Jones, Professor Paul Boreham, and Professor Stephen Bell. Second, warm thanks go to Dr. Brendon O'Connor, Dr. Matt McDonald, Dr. Morgan Brigg, Dr. David Hundt, Dr. John Mackenzie, Dr. Barbara Sullivan, and Miss Jenny Gall for their advice and encouragement. Third, I would like to thank Professor Ahmed Hamza and Professor David Kirby at The British University in Egypt for their generous support of my academic endeavours. Fourth, thanks go to Farideh Koohi-Kamali, Robyn Curtis, and Erin Ivy at Palgrave Macmillan for their guidance, patience and professionalism. My gratitude to all those who extended hospitality to me on my travels through Indonesia and helped bring its beautiful diversity to life. Finally, to friends and family, my heartfelt thanks for the emotional support necessary to complete this book. You know who you are.

LIST OF ABBREVIATIONS

ABRI	Angkatan Bersenjata Republik Indonesia (Armed Forces of the Republic of Indonesia)
AMIN	Angkatan Mujahideen Islam Nusantara (Nusantara Islamic Jihad Forces)
AFC	Asian Financial Crisis
APPI	Asosiasi Partai-Partai Islam (Association of Islamic Parties)
BIN	Badan Intelijen Negara (State Intelligence Agency)
BI	Bank Indonesia
BKI	Badan Penyeliduk Usaha Persiapan Kemerdekan Indonesia (Committee for the Investigation of Independence)
BLBI	Bantuan Likuiditas Bank Indonesia (Bank Indonesia Liquidity Assistance)
BPK	Badan Pemeriksa Keuangan (Supreme Audit Agency)
COHA	Cessation of Hostilities Agreement
Bulog	Badan Urusan Logistik Nasional (National Logistics Agency)
DDII	Dewan Dakwah Islamiyah Indonesia (Islamic propagation council of Indonesia)
DI	Darul Islam (Abode of Islam)
DPR	Dewan Perwakilan Rakyat (People's Representative Council)
DPD	Dewan Perwakilan Daerah (Regional Representatives Council)
FDI	Foreign Direct Investment

FKAWJ	Forum Komunikasi Ahlus Sunnah wal-Jama'ah (Forum for Followers of the Sunna and the Community of the Prophet)
FPI	Front Pembela Islam (Islamic Defender Front)
GAM	Gerakan Aceh Merdeka (Free Aceh Movement)
Golkar	Golongan Karya (Functional Groups—the New Order state machinery)
HDC	Henry Dunant Centre
HMI	Himpunan Mahasiswa Islam (Muslim Students' Association)
IBRA	Indonesian Bank Restructuring Agency
ICMI	Ikatan Cendekiawan Muslim Indonesia (Association of Muslim Intellectuals)
JI	Jemaah Islamiyah (Islamic Community)
KAMMI	Kesatuan Aksi Mahasiswa Muslim Indonesia (United Action of Indonesian Muslim Students)
KISDI	Komite Indonesia Untuk Solidaritas dengan Dunia Islam (Indonesian Committee for Solidarity of the Islamic World)
KPK	Komisi Pemberantasan Korupsi (Corruption Eradication Commission)
KPU	Komisi Pemilihan Umum (General Election Commission)
KUII	Kongres Umat Islam Indonesia (Congress of the Indonesian Islamic community)
LBH	Lembaga Bantuan Hukum (Legal Aid Institute)
LJ	Laskar Jihad (Army of Jihad)
LMI	Laskar Mujahidin Indonesia (Indonesian Mujahidin Militia)
LPI	Laskar Pembela Islam (Defenders of Islam Army—para-military wing of FPI)

MMI	Majelis Mujahidin Indonesia
	(Indonesian Mujahidin Assembly)
MPR	Majelis Permusyawaratan Rakyat
	(People's Consultative Assembly)
MUI	Majelis Ulama Indonesia
	(Council of Indonesian Ulama)
NII	Negara Islam Indonesia
	(Indonesian Islamic State)
NU	Nahdlatul Ulama
	(Islamic social organization)
PAN	Partai Amanat Nasional
	(National Mandate Party)
PBB	Partai Bulan Bintang
	(Crescent Star Party)
PBN	Partai Buruh Nasional
	(National Labour Party)
PD	Partai Demokrat
	(Democratic Party)
PDI	Partai Demokrasi Indonesia
	(Indonesian Democratic Party)
PDI-P	Partai Demokrasi Indonesia—Perjuangan
	(Indonesian Democratic Party—Struggle)
PK	Partai Keadilan
	(Justice Party)
PKB	Partai Kebangkitan Bangsa
	(National Awakening Party)
PKI	Partai Komunis Indonesia
	(Communist Party of Indonesia)
PKPB	Partai Karya Peduli Bangsa
	(Concern for the Nation Party)
PKPI	Partai Keadilan dan Persatuan Indonesia
	(Indonesian Justice and Unity Party)
PKS	Partai Keadilan Sejahtera
	(Justice/Welfare Party)
PKU	Partai Kebangkitan Ummat
	(Muslim Nation Awakening Party)
PMB	Partai Masjumi Baru
	(New Masjumi Party)

PNI	Partai Nasional Indonesia (Indonesian Nationalist Party)
PPBI	Pusat Perjuangan Buruh Indonesia (Indonesian Centre for Labour Struggle)
PPI	Partai Pekerja Indonesia (The Indonesian Workers' Party)
PPP	Partai Persatuan Pembangunan (United Development Party)
PRRI	Pemerintah Revolusioner Republik Indonesia (Revolutionary Government of the Republic of Indonesia)
PSI	Partai Sosialis Indonesia (Indonesian Socialist Party)
PUDI	Partai Uni Demokrasi Indonesia (Democratic Unity Party: Indonesia)
PUI	Partai Ummat Islam (Muslim Believers' Party)
REPLITA	Rencana Pembangunan Lima Tahun (Five-year development plan)
TNI	Tentara Nasional Indonesia (Indonesian National Defence Forces)

GLOSSARY

abangan	nominal Muslim
adat	traditional custom
aliran	stream or flow of certain ideas, thinking, and ways of life
aliran kepercayaan	formal expression of *kebatinan*
budaya petunjuk	culture of obedience
bupati	regency/district head
camat	subregency head
cukong	ethnic Chinese financial backers
desa	village
dwifungsi	dual function of the Indonesian armed forces
gotong royong	mutual cooperation
gusti	aristocratic lord
hadrami	Indonesians of Middle Eastern descent
Iskandar Muda	twelfth Sultan of Aceh (1583–1636)
jasa	service-mindedness
kabupaten	regency
kampung	urban neighbourhood, often slums
kawula	subject
kebatinan	religiously syncretic Javanese beliefs (Javanism)
kecamatan	subregency
kekeluargaan	society as one family with the state as head of the family
kelurahan	administrative unit below *kecamatan,* comprising several *desa*
kepala desa	village head
keterbukaan	political openness
khittah	social-religious identity
kyai	religious leader and expert in Islam
lengser keprabon	to step down from power

lurah	district head or historically a village leader especially in Java
Masjumi	pre–New Order Islamic political party
mufakat	consensus
Muhammadiyah	Islamic social organisation
musyawarah	deliberation
Orde Baru	New Order (1965–1998)
Orde Lama	Old Order (1945–1965)
pamrih	concealed self-interest
Pancasila	official national ideology of the Republic of Indonesia
Pertamina	Indonesia State Oil Company
pesantren	Islamic boarding school
politik aliran	communitarian or "stream" politics organized around affiliation and allegiance to particular *aliran*
pribumi	ethnic Indonesians
reformasi	reformation
Shari'a	Islamic religious law
ulama	body of Islamic leaders
wahyu	unifying power of a ruler
wong cilik	little people or the masses

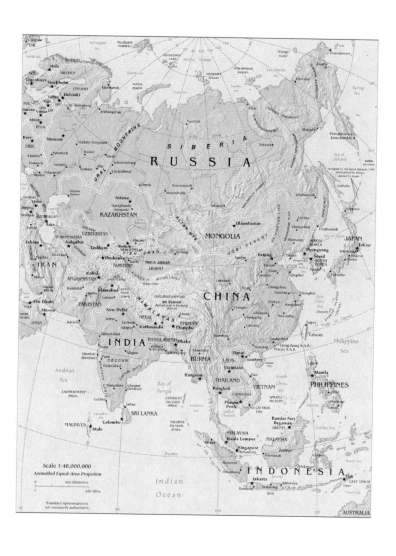

ARCTIC Ocean

NORWAY
Oslo
SWEDEN
Copenhagen
Stockholm
FINLAND
Helsinki
Murmansk
POL.
Warsaw
BELA.
Minsk
Kiev
UKR.
Kharkiv
Moscow
Voronezh
Nizhny Novgorod
Kazan
Ufa
Perm
Yekaterinburg
Chelyabinsk
Omsk
URAL MOUNTAINS
SIBERIA
RUSSIA
Krasnoyarsk
Novosibirsk

Astana
Qaraghandy
(Karaganda)
KAZAKHSTAN
UZBEKISTAN
Tashkent
Bishkek
TIEN SHAN
Almaty
ALTAI MTS
MONGOLIA
Ulaanbaatar
GOBI DESERT

IRAN
Tehran
TURKMENISTAN
Ashgabat
Dushanbe
TAJIKISTAN
TAKLA MAKAN
DESERT
KUNLUN MOUNTAINS
CHINA
Beijing
NORTH
KOREA
Pyongyang
Seoul
SOUTH
KOREA
JAPAN
Tokyo
Osaka
Vladivostok

AFGHANISTAN
Kabul
Islamabad
Lahore
PAKISTAN
New Delhi
HIMALAYAS
Mt Everest
NEPAL
Kathmandu
BHUTAN
Thimphu
Lhasa
Chengdu
Chongqing
Wuhan
Shanghai

Karachi
Ahmadabad
Jaipur
Lucknow
Kanpur
INDIA
BANGLADESH Dhaka
KOLKATA
(Calcutta)
BURMA
Mandalay

Mumbai
(Bombay)
DECCAN
Hyderabad
Bangalore
Chennai
(Madras)
Bay of
Bengal
Rangoon
THAILAND
Bangkok
LAOS
Vientiane
Hanoi
VIETNAM
Ho Chi Minh
City
CAMBODIA
Phnom
Penh
Gulf of
Thailand
Manila
PHILIPPINES
Philippine
Sea

Arabian
Sea
LACCADWEEP
(INDIA)
Cochin
Jaffna
SRI LANKA
Colombo
MALDIVES
Male
ANDAMAN
ISLANDS
(INDIA)
NICOBAR
ISLANDS
(INDIA)

Indian
Ocean

Scale 1:48,000,000
Azimuthal Equal-Area Projection
0   900 Kilometres
0   600 Miles
Boundary representation is
not necessarily authoritative.

MALAYSIA
Kuala Lumpur
Singapore
Medan
MALAYSIA
Borneo
Bandar Seri
Begawan
BRUNEI
Celebes
Sea

INDONESIA
Jakarta
Java
Surabaya

Dili
EAST TIMOR

AUSTRALIA

PART I

INTRODUCTION

In 1991, Samuel Huntington identified a "Third Wave" of democratization. This wave emerged in Southern Europe in the 1970s and swept across vast swathes of the developing world in the 1980s and 1990s, analyses of which gave us a democratic transition paradigm of three phases. First, the "opening," a period of liberalization during which the authoritarian regime weakens. After that, "breakthrough," where the old regime suffers a crisis of legitimacy, starts to unravel, and a more liberal system begins to emerge. Finally, the "consolidation" period should ideally usher in reforms in state institutions and practices that facilitate progress toward a stable and strong democracy.

Yet, in the intervening years since the Third Wave surge, experience tells us that democratization is as susceptible to breakdown as consolidation (Bunce 2000: 703–734; Whitehead 2002). New institutional rearrangements often stall as countries retreat into what Marina Ottoway (2003: 3) has termed a "semi-authoritarian" condition. In fact, it seems that the transition paradigm is struggling for purchase on shifting sands (Carothers 2002: 5–21). As it stands today, democratization is more a case of ambiguous transformation than predictable outcome.

Evidently, how and why democratic institutions become established and accepted (or not, as the case may be) remain difficult questions to answer. This leaves observers of the phenomenon facing a number of challenges. To start with, the nonlinearity of democratization stubbornly resists straightforward explanation. We cannot simply assume that political agency operates in an unimpeded manner or that structural circumstances directly determine matters. Rather, the alteration and reconstitution of disarticulated political space is a form of (re)negotiation between culture and politics and of that between discourse and practice. That is to say, a country's societal conventions, cultural practices, and developmental legacies affect an evolving postauthoritarian grammar of political action. At the same time as human actors, transform structural factors into resources for change (Kim, Liddle, and Said 2006: 247–268).

As such, decisions enacting change are not always necessarily the best, or even the most rational. Just as Luigi Pirandello's ([1921] 1952) characters were in search of an author, similarly, during democratization, political actors old and new are looking for redefined roles. Although they compete against each other to establish the new rules of the political game in their favor, compromises do take place. This dialectic uncertainty creates a disjuncture in the social causality of both structural and rational choice approaches and their explanation of political change. We are left trying to thread a narrative along what is a very uneven road from authoritarianism to democratization. This is no easy task, because it involves unravelling both the material and discursive practices of a process in which political actors enact the democratization they ultimately constrain.

This is why this book is not only about Indonesia but also about concepts. It seeks to (re)conceptualize the Indonesian road to democratization in a nonteleological manner. Our story here is not strictly one of opening, breakthrough, and consolidation but of political compromise. The book attempts to take us beyond the binary realms of unimpeded political agency and preconditioned social conflict by establishing how and why interpreting ambiguity matters in the study of Indonesian democratization. In tracing an enacting grammar of political action, this book frames Indonesia's postauthoritarian settlement as a political (re)negotiation between history, culture, and identity. This brings the unevenness of Indonesia's journey from authoritarianism to democratization into view.

To elaborate, in the wake of Suharto's downfall in 1998, Indonesia embarked upon a significant democratic transformation. The *reformasi* (reformation) period represented a critical moment in Indonesia's postindependence history. Having said this, although the initial tide of reform brought new rules to the political game, the specter of oligarchy continued to haunt new institutional reconfigurations. There was an "appearance" of more open politics, but some commentators drew the conclusion that Indonesian democratization was actually reinscribing oligarchic rule instead of transforming it democratically. For instance, the commendable work of Vedi Hadiz (2003: 593) highlighted the ability of Indonesian oligarchs "to reinvent themselves through new alliances and vehicles, much like they have, for example, in parts of post-Communist Eastern Europe/Central Asia."

While not wanting to deny oligarchic persistence, I feel the latter conclusion relies too heavily on the assumption that institutional outcomes are a direct and causally contingent struggle between salient socioeconomic forces. The reality seems to be far more ambiguous. In fact, Indonesia continues to not only reorganize but transform and regenerate. If we are to unravel this process, identifying the manner in which political actors draw upon and reinvent traditional identifications is an important step. The reason being, as Benedict Anderson (1991) draws attention to, people who perceive themselves as part of a political community ultimately imagine it. The nation is, therefore, a social construct that rests upon a process of invention and reinvention of traditions. In these terms, Indonesia's contextual narratives are the constitutive substance of perception and provide symbolic resources to political actors from which they can legitimate a postauthoritarian grammar of political action. By exploring the ambiguous interplays between authoritarian legacies of the past, communitarian politics (*politik aliran*), Islamic identification, emerging middle classes, popular protest, and decentralization reforms in Indonesia, this book points to reconfigured patterns of politics that are emerging.

BOOK ORGANIZATION

This introduction has briefly outlined the rationale behind the book and its main objectives. The intent is to advance a rigorous multidimensional framework for interpreting ambiguity in democratization and apply this in more detail to an mapping of Indonesia's journey from authoritarianism.

To start with, Chapter One establishes the relationship between democratization and ambiguity by reviewing the major schools of thought and key conceptual issues in the field. This led me to conclude that a multidimensional framework is best suited to investigate the ambiguous interplay between structural context and political agency in the study of democratization. Chapter Two builds on this framework by identifying a number of significant and interrelated contextual narratives that evolved in Indonesia prior to 1998. It considers their affect on political action and establishes that ideational resources exert not only a play of selective constraint but constructive potential. Chapter Three furthers the analysis by examining the extent to which the (re)emergence of symbolically embedded political culture informs Indonesian democratization and whether it offers a viable means for representing a modern heterogeneous society.

Chapter Four then explores the ways in which Indonesia's Islamic identification informs its democratization and the extent to which the new democratic framework accommodates a diversity of contemporary Islamic political expression. Chapter Five utilizes the economic developments outlined in Chapter Two to examine the rise of the Indonesian middle classes and their role in democratization before and after 1998. Chapter Six maps Indonesia's post-authoritarian party system to weigh up whether popular protest translated into representative capacity.

Chapter Seven (a version of which originally appeared in Pacific Affairs vol. 81, no. 4 [Winter 2008/2009]) draws together the themes from the preceding chapters and examines the effect of decentralization on the highly centralized state structures of the Suharto era. It considers the extent to which a politico-institutional variable can destabilize asymmetries of political power and influence the evolving political process. Chapter Eight concludes this inquiry into how and why things rarely unfold as we would want them to.

PART II

FRAMEWORK FOR INTERPRETING AMBIGUITY IN DEMOCRATIZATION

CHAPTER 1

DEMOCRATIZATION AND AMBIGUITY

The future stability and expansion of the democratic project has been a major issue in the international community since the end of the Cold War. As Larry Diamond (2003: 1–25) notes, in 1974, there were 41 democracies among the existing 150 states, and by 2001, 121 of 193—or about three-fifths of all states—were considered formal democracies. Yet, Thomas Carothers (2002: 5–21) had earlier drawn our attention to the fact that out of nearly 100 transitional countries, probably less than 20 were well on their way to becoming successful, well-functioning democracies, mainly in Central Europe and the Baltic region with a few in South America, Asia, and Africa. In fact, recent ambiguous advances mean it is becoming harder to reach a consensus in the field of study about an adequate explanation of democratization.

This lack of consensus seems to arise in no small part from the analysis of democratization itself. What we confront are two approaches broadly framing the subject of inquiry, namely structural and actor-centric. Each approach influences assumptions made, interpretations applied, and conclusions reached, out of which disagreement is sure to follow. Of more concern, however, is the fact that our framing of democratization in terms of a structure and agency binomial is counterproductive. First, experience tells us that neither structure nor a free-play of unconstrained political agency predetermines democratic change in exclusivity. This is something that stretches each approach's ideas of causation and conceptual closure to their limits. Second, the process is far more ambiguous in terms of institutional outcomes than either approach presumes. This is evidenced by the unexpected patterns of institutional transformation and distinct trade-offs that have occurred over the years (Munck 1993: 475–498; Whitehead 2002: 2–3). It seems that the two approaches both find it difficult to grasp the protean nature of democratization. Paradoxically, the ambiguity of change leaves them sitting somewhat uncomfortably with the actuality of contemporary postauthoritarian settlements.

One of the challenges facing researchers of democratization is, therefore, to reconcile the analytic tension between paradigmatic assumptions and ambiguous advances. The following chapter addresses this challenge by, first, examining the major schools of thought on transition and consolidation for key epistemological and methodological clues. Second, equipped with coordinates from the extant literature, the chapter tentatively outlines a conceptual framework for mapping ambiguity and relating it to Indonesia's postauthoritarian settlement.

CONCEPTUAL TRAVAILS FOR A COMMON PURPOSE

Samuel Huntington (1991) in his taxonomy of global democratic change identified various waves of democratization.

The first wave had started with the revolutions in the Americas around the nineteenth century and ended with new democracies at the end of World War I. A second wave coincided with the Allied victory in 1945 and decolonization. The Third Wave broke with the demise of dictatorships in Spain, Greece, and Portugal between 1974 and 1976 and swept across numerous countries in a remarkable fashion. Although far from perfect, the Third Wave of democratization from the 1970s to the 1990s challenged many earlier assumptions about the process, especially the relationship between democracy and development. The inference seems to be that despite numerous reversals and even though democracy takes many different forms, more nations are turning toward some form of popular representative government. For example, despite clear differences between the institutional arrangements and practices of say Costa Rica, Estonia, or Ghana, all are democratic. This is where it gets interesting, because democratization, whether at the political or social level, is multilayered and complex. As Juan Linz and Alfred Stepan (1996: 5–14) argue, if democracy is to become the "only game in town," then change has to occur on the behavioural, attitudinal, and constitutional levels. This obviously means more than just elections. Institutional developments do need to take place in both political and civil society before democratic practices and values become entrenched and accepted. Not only does this present a major challenge in practical terms but also, without detailed conceptual articulation, we run the risk of applying excessive universalism to a manifold phenomenon.

We, therefore, need to work out what democratization is and is not. The following section outlines a broadly accepted procedural understanding of democracy and the necessary considerations in framing Indonesian democratization.

To start with, we can be sure that democratization is not the equivalent of democracy. The latter is a political system while the former is the process of establishing that system. But having said this, in most cases the democratization literature adopts a procedural view of democracy to frame its subject of inquiry for measurement purposes. As Barbara Geddes (1990: 131–150) points out, this establishes a reasonable "cut-off" point for distinguishing between democratic and nondemocratic regimes. If we were to utilize too substantive a definition of democracy, we would find it difficult to establish a reasonable number of new democracies to study. We would, in effect, incapacitate our attempts to identify significant, if incomplete, democratic change in the political realm (Karl 1990: 2–3). This is where Robert Dahl (1971) comes in handy. Dahl's definition of a modern functioning democratic polity (polyarchy) allows us to discern a democratic from a nondemocratic regime. And if we can identify certain formal characteristics, then we can approach our subject of inquiry in a consistent and reasonably parsimonious manner. Substantive limitations aside, it does give us a commonly agreed upon basis to analyze a set of identifiable criteria as follows:

- Elected officials, rather than unelected elites, have constitutionally vested control over government decisions on policy.
- Elected officials chosen in free and fair elections in which coercion is comparatively uncommon.
- Practically all adults have the right to vote in the election of officials.
- Practically all adults have the right to run for elective office.
- Citizens have a right to express themselves on broadly defined political matters without risk of severe punishment.

- Citizens have the right to seek out alternative sources of information.
- Citizens have the right to form relatively independent associations and organizations.

What this checklist indicates is that for contemporary politics to operate effectively (with multiple political elites working in both contestation and compromise with one another) certain broadly defined civil and political checks and balances are required. There is little point in assuming that elections in isolation will simply channel political action into peaceful contests among elites and accord public legitimacy. There has to be correspondent development of referable state institutions, societal behaviour, and policy-making procedures. To make this effective, a political system has to take on certain formal characteristics, that is, elected officials, free and fair elections, inclusive suffrage, the right to run for office, freedom of expression, alternative information, and associational autonomy (Dahl 1989: 221).

With this set of criteria in mind, Guillermo O'Donnell (1996: 35–36) also offers some important advice on deciding whether a regime is successfully on the road to democratic change or not. First, there should be no arbitrary termination of elected and appointed officials from office before the end of their constitutionally mandated terms. Second, elected officials should not be subject to severe constraints or exclusion from certain policy domains by nonelected actors. Third, the national territory should be inclusive of the voting population. Fourth, there should be an expectation that a fair electoral process and its surrounding freedoms will continue into an indefinite future.

Having established a working definition of democracy to ground our inquiry, the next important thing to remember is that democratization is not the same thing as democracy.

Democracy is the political system, but democratization is the process of changing a regime type and institutionalizing that political system. Our definition of democracy identifies the political system, but our definition of democratization identifies the political development that changes a prior authoritarian regime and institutionalizes a democratic political system. This distinction may seem theoretically pedantic, but it carries considerable implications. As Geddes (1990: 131–150) notes, whatever we believe to be constitutive components of democracy will determine, in certain respects, our thinking about how a political system democratizes because these components are the ones that need to be present for us to categorize a regime as a democracy. What we have here is a recipe for confusion and contestation about the causes and consequences of democratization (Collier and Levitsky 1997: 430–445).

On an institutional level, at least, there is a difference between a political system and the process of establishing that system. Normative ideas of democracy may help define political systems policy makers seek to establish, but this tells us little about what we need to know to establish those systems. To do that we need to focus on dynamics and how democratic institutionalization works, that is, the process of establishing a political system. This is because human actors who shape matters in particular settings are the ones who turn structural factors into political resources for change (Kim, Liddle, and Said 2006: 247). And it is through their efforts to bring about institutional reform that an organizational context exists with the potential to cultivate different behaviour and promote more representative and competitive politics. The establishment of an institutionalized democratic process, therefore, takes political decisions on, amongst other things, new constitutional arrangements, the rules of future political competition, and the dismantling of the structures of authoritarian rule. In analytic terms, as Adam Przeworski (1991: 26) notes, our concern should focus on the process by which relevant political actors find out how best to continue to submit their interests and values to the uncertain interplay of democratic institutions.

This is no straightforward task, because there is no direct, unmediated, or irreversible shift from regime A to regime B. The process is as prone to breakdown as progress. There is also the possibility that political actors will favor certain interests and familiar arrangements. In other words, the decisions made by political actors during democratization are not without baggage. A connection exists between preferences, capacities, and conditions in which they appeared. It plays a significant part in future developments. Add on the fact that a chain of events can also alter a country's dynamics of change and an easy explanation of democratization seems unlikely. As Laurence Whitehead (2002: 2–3) rightly notes, democratization resists the attention of a single paradigmatic lens. This is in large part due to the high levels of uncertainty and indeterminacy associated with the process (Mainwaring et al. 1992: 332).

To elaborate, democratization necessarily involves new actors, rules, practices, and perhaps even new values and resources, but not everything changes when a polity shifts into the process. That is to say, democratization does not unfold in a vacuum. Countries that enter a process of democratization already vary on the institutional, political, economic, and sociocultural levels that in turn affect their dynamics of change. As a result, research frameworks are constantly struggling to deal with changing realities that test received theoretical assumptions. With these considerations in mind, a good first step toward investigating this inherently indeterminate process would be to situate the contributions from the major schools of thought and the issues that arise in the study of democratization.

Modernization School

In the early years of this field of study, influential initial expressions came from the likes of Seymour Martin Lipset (1959), Walt Rostow (1960), and Alexander Gerschenkron (1962). Their work emphasized that democracy was more likely to emerge in countries with higher levels of socioeconomic development. By claiming that democratic breakthrough arose from the level of modernization in a country, this drew broad correlations between economic development and political change. The underlying assumption was that economic development led to regime differentiation and development of a civil society thus providing the foundations for a viable democracy. This implied a causal link between Western forms of development and the diffusion of liberal-democratic political culture across less developed countries and the subsequent democratic breakthrough. The more developed a country, the less chance of structurally conditioned social conflict with democratization being the final stage of a process of differentiation and specialization, industrialization, urbanization, secularization, and individualization. On a policy level, the dominant wisdom of the time was for developing countries to adopt Western economic and social patterns to ensure democratic political development.

The idea of linear acculturation meant that the identification of prerequisites for democracy became a key focus of this early research. Unfortunately, what it tended to ignore was the actuality of cultural difference and contingent historical experience. These factors played crucial roles in eventual outcomes. Indeed, Huntington (1965), Dankwart Rustow

(1970), and Dahl (1971) were all quick to recognize that a country's own distinctive institutions affect regime change. As Huntington (1965: 386–430) noted, the outcome of economic development was at least as likely to be political decay, instability, and authoritarianism. Having said this, Huntington (1991) did later argue that wealthier developing countries are more likely to be democratic. Other studies, most importantly Przeworski, Michael Alvarez, Jose Cheibub, and Fernando Limongi (2000), suggest that socioeconomic conditions do not prevent democratic breakthrough. The caveat being that once a breakthrough occurs such conditions do dramatically affect the quality of political democracy that establishes itself. It is reasonable to infer from this that transitions are unpredictable, but once achieved, countries can sustain them provided they achieve higher levels of GDP per capita with increased equitable distribution. This seems to point to the fact that there are a number of interrelated factors conducive to democratic persistence including higher rates of literacy, education, urbanization, and an independent media.

DEPENDENCY SCHOOL

The alternative perspective of the dependency school of thought cast doubt on the early optimism of modernization interpretations. This school attributed failure to democratize in large parts of the world to the global capitalist system itself. For the likes of Immanuel Wallerstein (1979), who followed a broadly Marxian analytic tradition, the ability of a developed "core" of Western states to exploit the cheap, unskilled labor and raw materials within and between "periphery" and "semi-periphery" localities kept them in a state of underdevelopment. Similarly, Andre Gunder Frank (1967) saw this as a reason why many developing countries failed to enjoy the fruits of their labor despite decades of following Western patterns of development. As Fernando Henrique Cardoso and Enzo Faletto (1979) noted, the structure of world trade and foreign investment resulted in more capital outflows than inflows in developing countries. Nicos Poulantzas (1976) and Nicos Mouzelis (1986) further concluded that Western-led modernization was harmful rather than beneficial to political development in these countries.

Having said this, the dependency school failed to explain why a Third Wave of democratization occurred despite the continuing peripheral economic status of many of the countries involved. In fact, the transitions in Southern Europe, Eastern Europe, and Southeast Asia between 1974 and 2000 highlighted the dependency school's overdetermined causality. Indeed, both modernization and dependency schools privilege the economic infrastructure as determining political outcomes. Yet, the work of Barrington Moore (1966) and Rustow (1970) demonstrates that the arbitrariness of economic preconditions makes it impossible to generalize them across all cases.

BUREAUCRATIC AUTHORITARIAN SCHOOL

As a palliative to structural overdeterminism, Huntington's (1968) work on praetorian political orders provided the groundwork to go beyond the explanatory rubric of preconditions. As Huntington (1968: 1–39) argued, political institutional developments were significant factors in explaining a lack of democratic development and authoritarian persistence. His work on the "isolated state" as a self-interested, autonomous actor had considerable explanatory appeal in the Southeast Asian context, where military coalitions perennially gained control of government apparatus. Indeed, you could view these countries as bureaucratic authoritarian regimes because military and civil service elites tapped into economic resources to service the state and their own interests.

For O'Donnell (1973: 6–8) modernizing elites ensured the rise of bureaucratic authoritarianism to protect their own interests and those of Western capital. This was a crucial factor in stalling democracy and propping up authoritarianism in Brazil after 1964 and in Argentina after 1966. In the latter cases, technocratic experts gave operational expression to the broad exclusionist practices of their military patrons. Similarly, for Mochtar Mas'oed (1989), this matched the dynamics of authoritarian persistence in Indonesia in the late 1980s. Yet, the rise of powerful and independent business classes throughout the 1980s left the bureaucratic authoritarian school of thought looking like a slightly overdetermined explanation. It failed to account for the intricacies of societies experiencing rapid growth and social change (Remmer 1982: 3–36). Interestingly, revised versions of this school of thought have undergone something of a revival in popularity in the study of hybrid or competitive authoritarian regimes.

STRATEGIC CHOICE SCHOOL

From the 1970s onward, in an attempt to bridge the dilemma of structural determinism, theorists started to explore political agency lines of inquiry. Rustow (1970: 337–363) began to question the earlier work of the modernization school and its search for prerequisites that centered around a consensus on civic culture and levels of economic development. He recognized that these were more likely the results of democracy rather than its causes. For Rustow, successful democratization rested on a gradual process of compromise. He understood that human agency affected this dynamic. Indeed, the handiwork of politicians skilled in bargaining techniques could create a pattern of compromise in the developmental process and facilitate transition.

Juan Linz and Alfred Stepan (1978), following on from Rustow, opened this new path further. Linz and Stepan (1978: 1–5) emphasized a more process-oriented perspective to account for the move from authoritarianism to democratic breakdown. In fact, the Third Wave of democratization challenged many of the earlier assumptions made about the relationship between democracy and development. Many of the transitions from the 1980s onward took place in countries with low levels of economic development and other less than favorable socioeconomic indicators. It seemed an economic development variable in exclusivity was insufficient to explain the timing of these democratic transitions and the complexity of the variables associated with them. Consequently, in their seminal four-volume work, O'Donnell, Schmitter, and Whitehead (1986: 71) adopted a strongly actor-orientated focus to account for the dynamics of transition. They saw it as neither logically nor historically possible to prove a structurally determined causal relationship between economic development and political change. This implied that stable democratic outcomes depended less on structural factors and more on the strategic interactions of principal actors involved during the transition (O'Donnell et al. 1986: 27–29). What we have here is a significant shift from a political economy of social conflict to explain change toward an analysis grounded in human agency, particularly elite political action. This highlighted the hitherto unexplored link between the strategic interactions of political elites and democratic transition.

As a result, O'Donnell et al. were able to draw distinctions between different types of authoritarianism and different types of transition. This allowed them to establish that authoritarianism in Southern Europe was more the product of right-wing political coalitions. As a form of *dicta blanda* (soft autocracy), it differed from the *dicta dura* (hard autocracy) of say Argentina. In Spain, for example, the ruling party played a subsidiary role to the ruling-class coalition. When they became an obstruction to coalition interests, the friability of authoritarian arrangements became all too apparent. This led to schisms between regime "hardliners" (*duros*) and "soft-liners" (*blandos*) (O'Donnell et al. 1986: 19). In Spain, Portugal, and Greece, the crumbling of consensus created internal crisis and the opportunity for conditional democratic compromise (O'Donnell et al. 1986: 27). In these terms, the pacts negotiated by political elites were more important to the success or failure of the transitions than structural preconditions.

For O'Donnell et al. (1986: 73), negotiations can also take different forms depending on the relative strength of the actors involved. A *ruptura pactada* can occur where there is a lack of political continuity with the prior regime. Alternatively, a *reforma pactada* can occur where there is an element of legal continuity with the prior regime, for example, the 1977 Pact of Moncloa in Spain between government, parliament, and trade unions. O'Donnell et al. (1986: 74) saw this as a template for a successful and stable transition. Either way, it is clear that the type of pact negotiated is crucial to the resultant postauthoritarian outcome. As Giuseppe Di Palma (1990) underlined, pacts bring stability as they allow the possibility of democratic coexistence. For Di Palma, establishing democracy was, in the main, a matter of proper crafting. From this perspective, if elite political actors commit to political change, then democracy can be possible despite adverse structural conditions. Having said this, since the 1990s, notable works by the likes of Stephan Haggard and Robert R. Kaufman (1995) and Dieter Rueschemeyer et al. (1992) have successfully balanced structural and agency-related factors to give nuanced accounts of transition dynamics.

PATH DEPENDENCY SCHOOL

In the early 1990s, path dependency emerged as a significant school of thought in the literature. Its central premise for studying democratization is that proximity to events of the day leads to a loss of perspective. Scholars like Ruth and David Collier (1991), Douglass C. North (1990), John Mahoney (2000), and Paul Pierson (2000) all introduced more diachronic perspectives into their work. Their work links the immediate catalysts of political instability with long-term factors of regime instability. This highlights the embedded nature of contingent transition phenomena in broader social dynamics. From a path dependency perspective, transitions are part of longer historical processes. In terms of democratization, critical junctures in a country's historical and institutional development shape its political arena. This in turn affects the prospects of political stability and future regime dynamics because historical and institutional junctures can trigger self-reinforcing feedback in a political system. That is to say, different historical contingencies can constrain and/or enable the choices political actors make and lead to different democratization paths. As such, a regime's historical antecedents provide important clues to the underlying forces at play, both internally and externally, in a particular setting.

Notably, continuity from a previous regime—and the degree and kind of political institutionalization—may lead different polities to produce different responses to the same set of exigencies. Although links to preexisting structures are neither straightforward nor specific across cases, a temporal sequence of events and processes shapes the political arena and influences the kind of democracy established. One cannot simply assume that political elites will "choose" democracy as the most rational option. Political actors have to make choices, but historical, cultural, and economic legacies constitute a context within which they must operate. That is to say, even with the advent of new institutional reform, underlying societal conventions, cultural practices, and authoritarian legacies can restrict, enhance, or predispose specific options. This in turn can produce distinct trade-offs and unexpected patterns of transformation and modification.

The path dependency school does more than fit appropriate cases into a modal pattern. By introducing an analytically coherent account of history, timing, and sequence in a nondeterministic manner, it shows how the feedback of economic context, historical structure, and political choices affects a country's democratization path. This provides a counter to some common misapprehensions by highlighting that differences are often too wide-ranging to generalize across the board. As we know, to paraphrase Kant, outcomes from the crooked timber of human activity are rarely straightforward.

To elaborate, when countries have different political institutionalization, sociocultural heritage, or economic fundamentals, thinking that they can achieve democracy in a manner that fully conforms to an abstract democratic norm is an unreasonable expectation. There are stark differences between the preceding regimes of say Eastern Europe and those of Latin America, Southern Europe, or East and Southeast Asia. State socialist regimes were different in relation to structure, ideology, political economy, civil-military relations, and position in the international system from other democratizers. State, nation, and identity were at the very centre of the transitions in Eastern Europe. Their change was simultaneously political and economic, while in Latin America and Southern Europe, the transformations were much more political in nature, with East and Southeast Asia falling somewhere in between. What this indicates is that to learn more about the nature of democratization, these differences demand detailed explication.

What is Democratic Transition?

What the major schools of thought highlight simultaneously is a contested field of study but one with common ground. Despite their differences, the schools readily agree that understanding the relationship between key stages—namely democratic transition and democratic consolidation—is crucial to understanding a country's overall process of democratization. However, there is also the recognition that articulating the relationship between these two distinct but interconnected phases is far from straightforward.

If we first consider democratic transition, we can identify a temporal phase of rapid change that can vary in length and uncertainty (Linz and Stepan 1978: 30–35). In its broadest sense, democratic transition begins with the breakdown of an authoritarian regime and ends with the initial establishment of some sort of democratic structures. According to Linz and Stepan (1996: 3), this phase is complete if "sufficient agreement has been reached about political procedures to produce an elected government, when a government comes to power that is the direct result of a free and popular vote, when this government de facto has the authority to generate new policies, and when the executive, legislative, and judicial power generated by the new democracy does not have to share power with other bodies de jure."

In an illuminating view of its macropolitical trajectory, Valerie Bunce (2000: 707) defines regime transition as a leap from "uncertain procedures and certain results" to "certain procedures and uncertain outcomes." What we have here is a gap of uncertainty between the breakdown of the previous regime (the entry into uncertainty) and the installation of a new regime (the exit from uncertain procedures to certain ones with uncertain outcomes). This is a fluid phase of opportunity and risk where the new institutional structures have not yet settled into a state of normality and residue from the old regime still exists. Of course, in these terms, it would be naïve to assume that democracy arises merely from the breakdown of the prior authoritarian regime. We know the point of departure, authoritarianism, but there is no way of knowing a priori the point of arrival. A liberal democratic outcome is far from a guarantee because the rules of the political game are still very much up for grabs. Political actors of varying persuasions are manoeuvring for the legitimate right to exercise control over public power and state apparatus (Linz and Stepan 1996: 14). Indeed, depending on the nature of the contest, a democratic transition can be suspended, wound back, or stalled as politicians struggle to define future rules and procedures (O'Donnell et al. 1986: 6).

There is also the effect of the actual mode of transition on future developments to consider. As Terry Lynn Karl and Philippe Schmitter (1991: 274) note

Transitions are "produced" by actors who choose strategies that lead to change from one kind of regime to another . . . they may be constrained by the choices available to them by prevailing social, economic and political structures and the interaction of strategies may often result in outcomes that no one initially preferred, but nevertheless we believe that actors and strategies define the basic property space within which transitions can occur and the specific combination of the two defines which type of transition has occurred.

In the 1970s, Dahl (1971: 45) predicted that, "in the future as in the past, stable polyarchies and near-polyarchies are more likely to result from rather slow evolutionary processes than from revolutionary overthrow of the existing regimes." Yet, with the advent of the Third Wave, the literature developed a useful shorthand to identify and consider the effects of different modes of transition. For Karl and Schmitter (1991: 261–284), there are four broadly agreed upon types of transition, which are revolution, imposition, reform, and pact. These range from the unilateral recourse to force through to a multilateral willingness to compromise. They correspond to a transition by revolution (Nicaragua 1979); transition by collapse (Greece and Portugal 1974); transfer of power (Bolivia 1978–1980); or negotiated regime-dominated transition (Spain 1974–1975 and Brazil 1978–1979). It seems the relative strength, control, or participation of the incumbent authoritarian leaders or opposition groups in the transition process are significant factors in future consolidation efforts (Munck 1994: 355–375).

As Linz (1990: 25–26) argues in relation to Portugal and Spain

> The political process subsequent to the installation of democracy differed decisively as a result of that initial step—coup d'etat versus reform. The role of different actors in the process could not be more different. And as a consequence, the party system, the position of the trade unions, the role of the armed forces, the relationship between the

new leadership and the men of the past etc., would also be different. The enactment of the Constitutions, the institutions created in that fundamental law, that has very important consequences for the political process, would also be quite distinct and pose different problems for the future.

For Donald Share, if a transition occurs because of regime collapse, "this . . . involves significant institutional changes and a rupture in the patterns of political authority" (1987: 532). On the other hand, in a transactional transition, "elites from the authoritarian regime initially control most aspects of the transition. Over time, the regime's control declines noticeably, but authoritarian elites still exercise greater capacity to shape the broad contours of the political process" (Share 1987: 533). As Mainwaring, O'Donnell and Valenzuela (1992) also note, the attitudes of the outgoing authoritarian elites and the relative strength of regime versus opposition actors can help determine aspects of the democratic consolidation phase.

These are no mere academic distinctions. As the Indonesian case reveals, its transition was one in which incumbent political elites maintained a level of control over the transition process. At the same time, they engaged in multilateral negotiation and compromise with the democratic opposition. The following chapters will establish how political elites largely agreed upon a multilateral compromise between themselves and the impact this had on the democracy that established itself. This form of elite-dominated transition differs from one imposed by incumbents without compromise with the opposition. Yet, it does not represent one in which mass actors exert a high degree of influence on the compromise between the opposition and the incumbent elites. Instead, in Indonesia, mass protests opened a political space for moderate opposition elites to exploit in the crafting of the new democracy.

As Karl (1990: 15) argues, this mode of transition affects consolidation because "[p]acted transitions are likely to produce corporatist or consociational democracies in which party competition is regulated to varying degrees determined, in part, by the nature of the foundational bargain."

This echoes Angelo Panebianco (1988: xiii), who recognized that the foundational moment of any new political arena is of paramount importance for subsequent development, even decades later. It may not necessarily define the future course of political development but lays the first bricks on which later politics builds.

WHAT IS DEMOCRATIC CONSOLIDATION?

Evidently, establishing institutional arrangements is one thing, sustaining them over time without their reversal is quite another. Moving on from the initial transition, therefore, involves a process of consolidation. But a different phase brings different problems. Institutionalization is more important during consolidation than transition. Consolidation involves not only the survival of a political democracy but also an element of sustainability. Famously, Linz (1990: 153) identified this as the requirement for democracy to become the "only game in town." It must become the institutional framework for regulating political life. As Schmitter (1992: 424) notes:

> The process of transforming the accidental arrangements, prudential norms, and contingent solutions that have emerged during the transition into relations of cooperation and competition that are reliably known, regularly practiced, and voluntarily accepted by persons or collectivities (i.e. politicians and citizens) that participate in democratic governance.

According to Gunther et al. (1996: 168), democratic consolidation occurs "when all politically significant groups regard its key political institutions as the only legitimate framework for political contestation, and adhere to democratic rules of the game." Likewise, for Przeworski (1991: 26), democratic consolidation takes place "when all the relevant political forces find it best to continue to submit their interests and values to the uncertain interplay of the institutions." Common to all these definitions is the recognition that consolidation involves the passage of time as the new set of rules for the political game are constructed and institutionalized.

Some scholars take a more critical stance by questioning the term "consolidation" and its implied definitional closure. They urge us to remain cautious about "attaching the term 'consolidated' to something that will probably though not certainly endure" (O'Donnell 1996: 38). In fact, the closure we ascribe to consolidation depends, in large part, on what point of the authoritarianism or developed democracy continuum we as observers choose to place ourselves. As Doh Chull Shin (1994) and O'Donnell (1996) both note, there is either explicitly or implicitly a requirement for a high degree of institutionalization and the establishment of formal procedural rules.

This assumption led O'Donnell (1996: 39) to argue that

> [t]his produces a tendency to push the conception of democracy in discussion of democratic consolidation towards an ideal, well-structured and comprehensive institutional system that can hardly be obtained, otherwise no regime is truly consolidated for the lack of an ingredient deemed essential and it is impossible to assign a reasonable closure to the second transition.

Indeed, John Markoff (1997: 68) reinforces the point by noting that "democracy is not a fixed entity, to be consolidated, but an invitation for further transformation, perhaps deepening and perhaps trivialising."

There is little doubt that there is a strong link between the consolidation phase and the transition period, but conditions that facilitate transition do not necessarily overlap with those that make democratic consolidation likely. According to Diane Ethier (1990: 140–165), factors affecting democratic consolidation include the mode of transition, the level of economic development, economic growth, the strength of civil society, and various institutional arrangements.

Somewhat differently, Geoffrey Pridham (1990: 103–117) argues that consolidation involves legitimization at both the elite and popular levels. There is a qualitative difference between transition and consolidation on political, economic, and civil society levels. It is clear that the dynamics of democratic consolidation and the key problems affecting it differ from the transition phase. In fact, to equate the breakdown of an authoritarian regime with a successful consolidation of democracy is a somewhat sanguine attitude to adopt. There is no simple linear progression from former to latter (Bermeo 1990: 359–377).

Having said this, there are a number of commonly agreed upon features. For Andreas Schedler (1998: 91–92), effective consolidations, to a large extent, have similar identifiable features: popular legitimization; the stabilization of electoral rules; judicial reform; the diffusion of democratic values; the marginalization of antisystem actors; civilian rule over the military; the removal of reserved authoritarian domains; party system development; the routinization of politics; and stabilization of the economy. In fact, democratic consolidation seems to depend on the willingness and capacity of a society to produce social and political structures capable of enduring and enjoying legitimacy. As Huntington (1991: 263) rightly points out, these developments take

time, that is, at least two successful elections and one transfer of power from incumbent to opposition.

HYBRID REGIMES AND THE END
OF THE THIRD WAVE

As mentioned in the introduction to this book, the transition paradigm is struggling for purchase on the shifting sands of reality. The most notable issue is an implicit
assumption that when a regime undergoes an "opening,"
it is inextricably moving away from authoritarianism toward
democracy. Experience tells us otherwise; it may be one
thing to establish formal democratic elections, but it is
quiet another to sustain them over time without reversal.
The work of the likes of Gretchen Casper (1995, 1996)
and Diamond (1997) both highlight that democratiz-
ing countries can drift in "protractedly unconsolidated"
states, seemingly unable to transform basic socioeconomic
orientations.

According to Schmitter (1994: 60), "democracy in its
most generic sense persists after the demise of autocracy, but
never gels into a specific, reliable, and generally accepted set
of rules." In extreme cases, extensive inherited constraints
can freeze the dynamics of change with a new regime stalling or simply reverting to a more or less semiauthoritarian/
oligarchic form of rule. Significantly, in recent years, as the
high watermark of the Third Wave receded and gave way
to a "fourth" wave of post-Communist African and Asian
transitions, we have witnessed some increasingly unusual
patterns of transformation or what could be termed, hybrid
regimes (Diamond 1996: 20–37; 2002: 21–36). Of course,
there have been some successful consolidations, but a stub-
born rump of illiberal forms of rule has emerged (Zakaria
1997: 22–43).

For instance, asymmetrical balances of power in places like Azerbaijan, Belarus, Kazakhstan, and Turkmenistan have produced some decidedly authoritarian outcomes. This seems to have been largely a consequence of the ideological orientations of decisive power holders during their transitions (McFaul 2002: 212–244). Moreover, in many hybrid cases, what we witnessed is a form of competitive authoritarianism emerging, where public officials often act to further their own interests at the expense of the public interest, that is, Cambodia and Nigeria. These countries may hold elections, but overall they simply lack many of the features that collectively define democracy. Often citizens have no real means of holding political elites to account beyond elections. They lack a sufficiently free press or the free associational autonomy to challenge malfeasance when it occurs. At the same time, an independent judiciary is usually a remote possibility that makes the rule of law an ineffective check. As a result, personalized interests go unchecked as the driving force behind the persistence of the hybrid regime with informal patronage networks and clientelistic structures running in parallel with formal institutions and high levels of corruption.

Irrespective of whether or not a regime is hybrid, frozen, or illiberal, what we do know is that transition and consolidation are difficult concepts to define and even harder to put into practice. Ad hoc or informal types of institutionalization may or may not settle, overtime, into more referable institutional arrangements. In fact, for many countries, consolidation is a very challenging process. With a bit of luck it comes more as an ex post facto realization than an adherence to formal criteria. But this raises important questions for academic inquiry. Most critically, who benefits from the new democracy and how representative is the political system? Answers to these questions involve moving beyond classification and attempting to understand how and why different countries end up the way they do and how their modes of governance affect their democratic settlement. One thing is for sure: our grasp on what makes for successful regime change will continue to remain elusive.

A FRAMEWORK FOR MAPPING AMBIGUITY IN INDONESIAN DEMOCRATIZATION

Clearly, the extant literature contains considerable strengths, with most investigations shining bright light on the dynamics of democratization. In fact, there seems little advantage in viewing different schools of thought pejoratively. They all contribute to the common search for answers in an intelligent manner. Nonetheless, certain blind spots remain in our understanding of democratization.

On the one hand, structural approaches tend to identify the causal narrative of democratic change with impersonal economic and technological forces. Forces that spread market-based social relations create new social identities that lead to the development of different outlooks. Despite an intuitive plausibility, this tends to overdetermine the analysis in terms of that causality. It establishes important economic developments but struggles to link regime-change dynamics, in a convincing manner, with the interplay between political agency and institutional development during transitions.

On the other hand, actor-orientated approaches view political choice as a crucial factor in democratic transitions and, therefore, tend to focus on decisions taken at crucial stages by leading political actors. We can see that the influence of the latter approach may bring human agency to the fore, but it also struggles to explain contingent socio-historical factors that shape actors' choices. As Gerardo

Munck (1994: 360) notes, exclusive focus on political elite interaction runs the risk of screening out broader social factors involved in conditioning political change.

Similarly, when we downplay historical contingency, it tempts us to accept a form of political voluntarism (Bunce 1995: 124). In other words, our chain of causality becomes too reliant on the subjective choices of key actors and leaves long-term factors of political instability underconceptualized. This is despite the fact that historically constituted structures can both enable and constrain the range of options available to decision-makers. It seems naïve to think that things change in a free-play of unimpeded political agency. In other words, context is clearly important to future developments, something brought into stark relief by the anomalous character of democratization in the post-Communist context and East and Southeast Asian countries (Bunce 2000: 703–734).

What this indicates is that the establishment of democracy involves generative factors beyond the rational capacity of elites to bargain about clear-cut choices. The preferences and capacities of individuals embody a historical context that may predispose them to specific options. Rather than democratization being direct and unmediated, variations of time and context create the possibility of different paths in particular settings. The time and context within which a transition takes place is a significant part of future developments. As a result, modes of transition may appear similar, but subtle variations can create large differences in outcome.

For instance, the Indonesian transition has been no easy ride since 1998. Even after unprecedented sociopolitical change, the configuration of power relations seemed to favor oligarchic persistence (Slater 2006: 208–213). Indeed, a legacy of corporatist centralization was always going to make democratic rearrangement vis-à-vis political power a complicated affair (Hainsworth, Turner, and Webster 2007: 41–46; Turner, Podger, Samardjono, and Tirthayasa 2003). And the country continues to experience widespread corruption, and officials, especially the judiciary, remain open to bribery and graft (Davidson 2007: 75–99). This is hardly a unique situation because legacies of authoritarian rule can constrain a polity's rearticulation even as the old institutional structures unravel (Bermeo 1990: 359–377).

A central concern in examining transition dynamics in Indonesia is whether the new democratic institutions taking shape destabilize asymmetries of political power or are, a priori, the subaltern to powerfully entrenched oligarchy, patronage, and money politics. Certainly, the kind of democracy establishing itself exhibits patrimonial tendencies, but to postulate their causal primacy in shaping institutions is altogether more contestable. In fact, to rely on this constant conjunctive to understand transition dynamics is a somewhat unwieldy reification of the subject of inquiry. As such, it inadvertently consigns transitology and its focus on elite political activity to the dustbin of "outdated sociology" (Nordholt 2003: 551). This is despite the fact that decision-making and compromise have played crucial roles in steering courses for successful and stable transitions (O'Donnell, Schmitter, and Whitehead 1986; Di Palma 1990). It may seem a counterintuitive understanding of social change, but the pragmatic interactions of political elites smooth the renegotiation of new social contracts without undue social disturbance. Considering their implications is, therefore, integral to understanding the dynamics of regime change.

Having said this, it would be naïve to assume that things change in a free-play of unimpeded political-agency (Bunce 2000: 703–734). If we are to appreciate the significance of strategic interactions, "it is necessary to grasp that those making major political decisions are not operating from a tabula rasa, merely projecting the most feasible solutions" (Kirchheimer 1965: 974). Yet, their decisions "can alter power relations, set loose new political processes, and lead to different (if often unintended) outcomes" (O'Donnell 1986: 38). This means that the exclusionary practices of competing social forces do not guarantee that *plus ça change plus c'est la même chose* (the more things change, the more they remain the same).

One, however, does need to be aware that transitions are not linear affairs. Despite the formal political transformations brought about by the Third Wave, further democratic deepening is a challenging affair. New regimes can stall or revert in varying degrees to illiberal forms of rule. In fact, outcomes are more often than not ambiguous (Whitehead 2002: 2–3). This is because a connection exists between the preferences and capacities of political actors toward change and the conditions in which they appeared. How could it be otherwise? The past developmental patterns and underlying societal conventions in particular settings influence the emergence of distinct trade-offs and unexpected institutional transformations. In fact, it is probably fairer to say that the politics of pragmatic democratic change more often than not serve the interests of established elites. Yet, what we recognize here in a very Aristotelian way is that political activity constitutes stable futures from troubled pasts.

This is worth remembering given that the study of democratization is a focus on the process of establishing a political system. In sociological terms, what we begin to appreciate is that democratization is a constantly changing phenomenon in terms of time, context, and agency. Achieving democracy is, therefore, not a predetermined end-state but a long-term and somewhat open-ended outcome (Whitehead 2002: 3). However, one can still unwittingly adopt a "retrospective determinism" (assuming what did happen is what had to happen) or even worse, "presentism" (considering that the motives and perceptions of the past are the same as those of the present). If we are to appreciate the dynamics of change, it is necessary to grasp that the contexts of regime instability within which actors deploy statecraft involve different notions of state, nation, and identity. The past developmental patterns and underlying societal conventions that they confront influence the emergence of distinct trade-offs and unexpected institutional transformations.

Having said this, a constructive grammar of political action can transform structural context into political resources for institutional change. As a process of negotiation, this does not guarantee a predetermined end-state or one-way democratic progress. Rather, what it speaks to is the realization that political actors utilize a polity's language of self-understanding to imagine and reconstitute disarticulated political space. To make this observation, however, raises considerable issues. It points to the fact that social structures are not independent of the values and practices they govern. And the preferences and capacities of political actors do not exist independently from the conditions in which they appeared. If this is the case then we have to deal with some complex analytic considerations.

We have to consider not only the space within which change occurs but how political actors draw upon, reinvent, or transform traditional identifications and how others involved might interpret what occurs. Indeed, the manner in which political actors remember, imagine, or transform their roles has to appeal and respond to a mass audience accustomed to viewing politics through extant sociocultural-historical lenses. Although new political space

opens and new audiences emerge, the space and audience
operate within a symbolic context that is already present
and located at the level of the polity's relationship to itself.
This means that the interplay between an evolving grammar of political action and structural context can both
constrain and enable the rearticulation of political space.
The decisions made during democratization are, therefore,
not necessarily rational in the strictest sense but are more
an adaptation to changing political space.

Our ontological categorization, therefore, can no longer
remain a binary dualism between structure and agency.
Thinking in these terms creates a false dichotomy between
the material and the ideational. The dynamic is, in fact,
relational. Indeed, the difficulty in separating social fact
from social value calls for a different approach to the subject of inquiry. Rather than remaining fixed to a single
paradigmatic attitude, one should adopt a more integrative
approach (Pridham 2000: 5–38). Retaining an open sen-
sibility to our inquiries is essential if we are to unravel
the relationship between political action and context
in postauthoritarian settings. Synthesis and plurality are
the touchstones to understanding ambiguity in all its
guises.

Placing uncertainty at the very heart of democratization is an important step to take if this is to work. It helps
us to recognize that political change is a process that
occurs through time by way of contestation, destabilization, and differentiation. As a result, framing democratization as a political renegotiation between history, culture,
and identity gives us a framework for mapping the complexity of this process in a nonlinear manner. If we apply
this in a rigorous manner, then it may open up a pragmatic
route for mapping the unplanned effects and outcomes of
democratization.

Conclusion

Evidently, countries do not emerge in straightforward transitions from authoritarianism to multiparty democracy. There are often regressions, breakdowns, and unexpected patterns of transformation. That is to say, change is not a linear trajectory. There is no predetermined endpoint but rather a process of destabilization, alteration, contestation, and reconstitution. Any account of this process, therefore, faces a number of challenges. On the one hand, there is little doubt that pragmatic decision-making and compromise help stabilize what is an uncertain process. On the other, things do not pan out in an unimpeded play of political agency. Societal conventions, cultural practices, and developmental legacies all influence the shape of the postauthoritarian settlement.

In fact, what these two facets of democratization indicate is a dynamic and complex process. The process oscillates between uncertainty, continuity, and change. This resists simple categorization, but reflects and constructs its own specificity in a nonlinear manner. Institutional outcomes, therefore, arise as a matter of time and degree from a complex interplay between political agency and context. In other words, the pattern of democratic politics that emerges is a renegotiation between a country's own history, culture, and identity, and the political discourse and practice that enacts it. This reiterative interplay means that ambiguity is to democratization as push is to shove. In these terms, the introduction of a fine-grained reading of the relationship between agency and contextual narratives of history, culture, and identity in the process of democratization is a useful step to take in unraveling the ambiguity of Indonesia's postauthoritarian settlement. The following chapters place some flesh on the bones of this approach.

CHAPTER 2

DEMOCRATIZATION AND
CONTEXTUAL NARRATIVES

On a conceptual level, the previous chapter established a framework for investigating the relationship between democratization and ambiguity in Indonesia. It sketched a mental road map of how political actors, old and new, transform structural circumstances into resources for change by selectively drawing upon symbolic narratives to form a grammar of political action. These discursive practices (the power of which is not necessarily tangible in the physical sense) set in motion a symbolic movement of interpretation and interpellation in the context of a particular setting. In other words, they provide a way of legitimating courses of action by appealing to a mass audience accustomed to viewing things through distinctive lenses.

As this chapter argues, identifying the particular contextual narratives in play during democratization can reveal important clues as to why things end up the way they do. Indeed, ambiguous outcomes arise in no small part because the political decisions enacting change involve compromises with the authoritarian past. The decisions are not necessarily the best, rather a case of what is possible given the circumstances. They reflect the renegotiation taking place between history, culture, and identity that simultaneously shapes the present reality. The following chapter maps out key contextual narratives in play before and after 1998: decolonization, nationalism, ideology, Islam, and patrimonial authority. Of course, the meaning of Indonesian democratization is not limited to these selected discourses, but their narrative threads provide a basis from which to understand the pattern of political compromise in Indonesia.

INDONESIAN NATIONALISM

A brief glance at Indonesia's geography and demographics tells us that any form of nationalism there will be a complex phenomenon. As the world's largest archipelago nation, it is host to vast diversity and consists of five main islands—Java, Sumatra, Sulawesi, Kalimantan (60 percent of Borneo), and Papua (western half of New Guinea) of which the Indonesian government declared Papua Barat (West Papua) a separate province in 2003. There are also 17,000 other smaller islands/islets with approximately 922 of these permanently inhabited. There are approximately 360 ethno-tribal groupings, 25 language groups, and over 250 dialects. Major ethnic populations include Javanese (41.71 percent); Sundanese (15.41 percent); Malay (3.45 percent); Madurese (3.37 percent); Batak (3.02 percent); Minangkabau (2.72 percent); and Betawi (2.51 percent).

Even with these bare statistics, it is easy to see that since independence, establishing a state capable of holding this diverse a conglomeration of peoples together has been a major exercise in nation building, especially in terms of integrative political identity. Fortunately, a shared history of anticolonial struggle has done much to help Indonesians imagine and construct normative values between state and society (Bertrand 2004). A shared national language (bahasa Indonesia) and state education system also helped foster this strong commitment to setting differences aside and working through problems.

To elaborate, Governor General Van Mook's attempt to revive the prewar plans of the Visman Commission ultimately floundered in the face of nationalist resistance. In 1947, when the Dutch tried to regain control over parts of the archipelago and isolate Republican forces through a federal solution, it met with forceful opposition. Indonesian independence leaders like Sukarno, Hatta, and Sjahrir deployed the idea of a single territorial unit of rule to mobilize the people around a progressive collective destiny. At the same time, they rejected Dutch economic interests, language, institutional symbols, and practices (Bertrand 2004: 28–29). These independence leaders utilized the term *perasaan senasib sepenanggungan* (the feeling of common fate and plight) to encapsulate their struggle and cast the Dutch as oppressors. This was a powerful discourse as it gave native peoples of the archipelago a narrative through which to recognize themselves as a community under colonial oppression and imagine something different. Later, under banishment by Suharto but in a similar vein, Pramoedya Ananta Toer's Buru Quartet (four semifictional novels that chronicle the development of Indonesian nationalism) gave strong voice to this transformative discourse.

Yet, as Mahmood Mamdani (1996) shows in the African context, colonial rule leaves a lasting impression with forms of rule locked into the shape of the postcolonial state by the European colonial powers that constructed that state. In preindependence Indonesia, for instance, the Dutch administrated the archipelago as a colonial state geared to extract revenues for their benefit. As Benedict Anderson (2001) argues, this meant that the Indonesian state in itself was a nineteenth-century colonial construct of defined boundaries. It was under Dutch rule that patterns of exploitative political, military, and economic practice firmly established themselves (Gouda 2000: 1–20). A major post-colonial legacy of the Dutch was, therefore, patrimonial networks of political elites who had acquired conditional power as colonial proxies. Local aristocracies had come to power as part of a Dutch strategy for co-opting local powerbrokers and enforcers. It was for them the most pragmatic way of maintaining order and control, a mechanism to regulate local relations that kept the indigenous population trapped in an ethnically ordered system.

The Dutch played an instrumental role in creating problematic race relations in Indonesia (Brown 1994). They maintained a strategic divide between Chinese Indonesians (*qiao sheng*) and native Indonesians (*pribumi*) by giving the former commercial and tax collection privileges. The Dutch effectively utilized them as an intermediary or comprador class. This policy unwittingly or otherwise served to fuel *pribumi* distrust and animosity toward Chinese Indonesians.

Consequently, during the postindependence Sukarno era, the goal of building a strong *pribumi* business class meant that the Chinese suffered political and economic marginalization. This remained largely the case in the Suharto era. But somewhat differently after 1965, prominent Chinese entrepreneurs who were cronies of Suharto like Liem Sioe Liong (Sudono Salim) and the Kien Seng (Mohammad "Bob" Hasan) also enjoyed regime patronage and became some of the richest men in Asia. Ordinary ethnic Chinese, on the other hand, experienced insidious discrimination under the New Order. Attempts by the New Order to forcibly assimilate and discriminate against the ethnic Chinese population in Indonesia are well known. The New Order effectively excluded ethnic Chinese from the military and politics and forced them into urban relocation. There was also pressure exerted on them to marry indigenous Indonesians, convert to Islam, and adopt Indonesian-sounding names (Schwartz 1994: 106). The coercive nature of this assimilation was evident in the discriminatory closure or nationalization of Chinese schools, the banning of Chinese literature, signs, and characters, the introduction of specially marked identity cards, and the imposition of legal restrictions on Chinese commercial activities.

PANCASILA

Repressive practices aside, in terms of national identity, Pancasila (panca—five; sila—principle) played a crucial unifying role for the fledgling republic. The Investigating Committee for the Preparation for Independence (BKI—Badan Penyeliduk Usaha Persiapan Kemerdekan Indonesia) helped in the formulation of this new national ideology that was later enshrined in Article 29, Section 1, of the 1945 Constitution. This ideology linked Indonesian national identity to five guiding principles of belief in one God, compassionate humanity, the unity of Indonesia, consensus democracy, and social justice. It was supposed to allow for the recognition of the diversity in Indonesian society while appealing to the greatest possible number of Indonesians. With his presidential power and ideas, Sukarno then utilized it as "a powerful myth of nationhood" (Mulder 1998: 121).

In the 1950s, the new national ideology became a potent political symbol for mobilizing the population and transcending societal cleavages. Sukarno united Indonesia's different cultures behind the common purpose of nation building. He also adopted the Malay of the islands as a national language (bahasa Indonesia). This was a clever choice as it avoided accusations of pro-Javanese bias. Having said this, the five interrelated principles of *bhinneka tunggal ika* (unity in diversity) loosely reflect traditional Javanese values and traditions. These symbolic markers included *musyawarah* (deliberation), *mufakat* (consensus), *kekeluargaan* (family), *manunggaling kawula* (unity of the ruler and ruled), and *gotong royong* (mutual cooperation). This form of solidarity infused the official national ideology with Javanese symbolism and cultural values. (Antlov 2000: 203–222). It also imbued the national political project with a consociation impulse representative of an image of a community that chooses a wise ruler by mutual consent. Further, Simanjuntak (1994) argues that the nationalist project shared similarities with Supomo's *negara integralistik* (an integrated state) put forward in 1945. Suharto would later reinterpret this idea for authoritarian ends with Supomo's *manusia seutuhnya* (whole man of humanity) to create his own *manusia seuthisuhnya pembangunam* (total Indonesian).

After the fall of Sukarno (1965–1966), Suharto retained key features of the nationalist project but took them in a decidedly authoritarian direction. There was a brutal purge of leftists with as many as 500,000 alleged communist sympathizers killed (Cribb 1990). Suharto also prohibited virtually all membership-based organizations autonomous of the government. This sweeping away of dissent paralysed the capacity for self-organization among the populace (Uhlin 1997). The New Order effectively decontested societal identity vis-à-vis the state by co-option and control. Of course, there were some notable exceptions in the form of Nahdlatul Ulama (NU—Awakening of Ulama) and Muhammadiyah, but this was on the condition that they did not agitate for political change.

In this repressive context, Pancasila survived as a useful legitimating grammar for Suharto's New Order regime, Orde Baru (1965–1998), largely due to its vague aspirations. Suharto was able to shift its common platform of unity into a full-fledged justification for his rule. By selectively reinventing Pancasila for development purposes, he was able to deploy it as the legitimating grammar for his brand of modernizing authoritarian corporatism. It provided a culturally symbolic justification for centralized authoritarian practices in order to achieve economic developmental goals (Bertrand 2004: 30–34).

This authoritarian interpretation of Pancasila slowly became a dominant political discourse (*bahasa pejabat*). Framing the legitimacy of the New Order around development rather than representation meant that repression, electoral intimidation, and control of the media could all be justified in the name of national interest. It provided Suharto with the political grammar to justify his prerogative and legitimate the enforcement of his guidance through various bureaucratic and ideological mechanisms.

Suharto also actively promoted the idea of a "floating mass" (*massa mengambang*) populace to further consolidate his rule. He infused the ideological foundations of his political project with corporatist ideas about organic integrated wholeness. By linking modernization with traditional Javanese cosmology, Suharto attempted to normalize New Order authoritarianism in the Indonesian imagination. Following New Order logic, a floating mass needed a paternal guide to steer them along the correct path. This symbolically infused logic tapped into and exploited cultural notions of obedience (*budaya petunjuk*).

The assemblage of which further reinforced traditional high Javanese notions of the little people (*wong cilik*) as ignorant (*masih bodoh*), whose place was to remain servile (*budak*) and obedient (*patuh*) to their ruler (*gusti*) and subordinate to the dominant class (*wong gede*), in this case, the controllers of the state apparatus.

With the New Order symbolically positioned, the state bureaucracy set to work utilizing various socialization techniques to establish its hegemony firmly in the popular imagination. Civil servants and community leaders followed programmes set up by the Agency for Pancasila Development (BP-7) and the Pancasila Promotional Programme (P-4). In addition, schools taught Pancasila moral education. Under the auspices of the New Order, Pancasila effectively became a normative projection of what the ruling elite deemed important and normalized their authority and rule in public discourse. This control of the interpretation and distribution of cultural knowledge allowed Suharto to construct a strong narrative structure around his corporatist vision.

Between 1983 and 1985, Suharto also banned any organization that failed to conform to Pancasila principles. This further corralled the populace into identifying with the patrimonial culture of the nation-state and the unifying power (*wahyu*) of Suharto. As we can see, the New Order cemented its control over political autonomy and economic policies through an ideological imbricate that privileged "state above politics." These discursive practices justified the legitimacy of state policies in the name of national interest (Robison 1986: 108). This is not to imply there were no voices of dissent, but they usually gained little traction against New Order hegemony. In May 1980, for instance, Petisi Limapuluh (the Petition of Fifty) criticized Suharto for redefining Pancasila to mean "loyalty to the president," but he quickly banned news coverage of the petitioners, prevented them from traveling, and withdrew government contracts from firms associated with them. As later chapters will discuss, this ideological socialization did much to undermine popular forms of opposition before and after Suharto's downfall.

ISLAMIC IDENTIFICATION

There is little doubt about the key role nationalism has played in the construction of Indonesian political identities. Yet, the centrality of religion to Indonesian life cannot be underestimated. The integration of religions, especially Islam, with indigenous belief systems has played a significant role in the history and cultural self-understanding of the archipelago. As a potential political resource, Islam has had a considerable influence on the language of Indonesian politics.

In the 1930s for example, whether Islam should constitute a foundational basis for the new state of Indonesia was the subject of intense debate between Agoes Salim, Natsir, and Sukarno. Natsir also pushed for the formation of a separate Muslim military unit. Indeed, since 1949, tension between Islam and the developing nationalist agenda has been evident in the history of the founding documents of the Republican movement. During the 1945 constitutional debates, Islamic groups proposed a preamble to this Constitution known as the Jakarta Charter. Stricter Muslims considered the Jakarta Charter as obliging the state to implement Islamic law across the Muslim community. Sukarno's decision to drop this preamble from the final constitution clearly reinforced the secular national project. Belief in one God became the first principle of Pancasila, but Article 29 of the preindependence 1945 Constitution gave the government the right to control and regulate religious life in Indonesia.

Over the years, these overlapping strands of national, religious, and cultural identity have created dynamic tensions within the political realm. First, the state, both in the colonial and postcolonial periods, has had an uneasy relationship with Islam and sought to curtail its political role. Second, this led to a three-way split in political ambitions of Islam as it evolved a variety of political/ideological responses to the Indonesian national project. The three most readily identifiable responses were traditionalist, modernist, and radical. The traditionalist response gave rise to NU, which is now a massive socioreligious organization boasting in the region of 30–35 million members. In the early years of the republic, the modernist Islamic party, Masjumi (the Council of Muslim Organizations), and its leaders played a prominent role in the short-lived parliamentary democracy. Indonesia's other main socioreligious organization, Muhammadiyah, views itself as the custodian of Masjumi's modernist Islamic legacy.

At the more radical end of the spectrum, revolutionary Islamic movements, Darul Islam (DI—Abode of Islam) and Tentara Islam Indonesia (TII—Indonesian Islamic Army), established vast guerrilla networks from the Islamic militias that had opposed the Dutch in Java. Sukarno banned both DI and TII from political participation, and by the 1960s, after sustained attack from the Indonesian military, they were in disarray. In fact, from the early 1950s onwards, Sukarno's nationalists had sought to depoliticize Islam as part of the national integrative project. In an attempt to weaken and divide Islam's political appeal, Sukarno strategically aligned with the moderate, social Islam of NU rather than the reformist Masjumi through his Nas-A-Kom project (Nationalis, Agama, dan Kommunis). This strategy marginalized Masjumi and eventually led to its collapse. Rising tensions between reformists like Natsir and traditionalists in NU escalated to the point where NU eventually seceded from Masjumi in 1952. Masjumi descended into factionalism in the run-up to the 1955 elections, and this effectively divided the Muslim electorate. It left the way clear for Sukarno and his nationalist party, Partai Nasional Indonesia (PNI), to register an emphatic triumph.

Thereafter, Sukarno abolished the *Konstituante* (Constituent Assembly—established to resolve the question of nation-state foundation) and reinstated the 1945 Constitution. This led Masjumi to boycott Djuanda Kartawidjaja's cabinet as a protest at its lack of accountability to parliament. In fact, Sukarno's guided democracy (*demokrasi terpimpin*) caused open rebellion as witnessed by the establishment of the Pemerintah Revolusioner Republik Indonesia (PRRI—Revolutionary Government of the Republic of Indonesia) in 1958. After the military quelled the rebellion, Sukarno jailed many of Masjumi's leaders for their PRRI involvement and eventually outlawed Masjumi in August 1960.

The ascendancy of Suharto in 1965–1966 brought with it widespread repression. As a result, Islam failed to recover the political influence it enjoyed in the early years of independence. Suharto sought to manage Islam for his own corporatist purposes and refused Masjumi the opportunity to return to the political stage. After 1968, he allowed Parmusi (the Indonesian Muslim Brotherhood) to form but effectively depoliticized Islamic organizations by bringing their interests under the umbrella of Partai Persatuan Pembangunan (PPP—United Development Party) in 1971. As a result, internal tensions beset PPP.

By the 1980s, NU had lost the Ministry of Religion, which represented a major symbol of its prestige and influence.

Abdurrahman Wahid (Gus Dur) realized that NU would have to play a more socioreligious (*khittah*) role and withdraw representatives from the New Order government. As the evidence suggests, the Indonesian Republic, from its inception, has both recognized and contained the political appeal of Islam. This leaves a tricky legacy for Indonesia because it now has to address the exclusionary practices that previously muffled its diverse Islamic communities.

CENTRALIZED PATRIMONIAL AUTHORITY

Having situated the depoliticization of Islam against the evolving nationalist project, we can now turn to another significant contextual narrative in Indonesia's political history, namely, patrimonial authority, a tendency that developed under Sukarno and became a defining feature of the Suharto era. The new nationalist leaders were keen to replace the Dutch, but proxy power vested through local practices is harder to undo. Familiar patterns emerged, whereby villagers supported local elites who in turn supported central elites in anticipation of reciprocal benefit (Antlov 1995).

To elaborate, the new political elite in Jakarta often made deals with local aristocracies, most notably in Bali, to ensure popular support for the fledgling republic and national project. Under Suharto, the centralization of authority intensified with local elites firmly attached by patronage networks to a highly centralized and hierarchical state power-base in Jakarta. Suharto ensured support for his leadership by using a mixture of fear and rewards with his collaborators in the state bureaucracy, business, and the military. As Harold Crouch (1979: 578) noted, "the New Order bore a strong resemblance to the patrimonial model.

Political competition among the elite did not involve policy, but power and the distribution of spoils." This dominance would eventually descend into a form of sultanism where power and resources were concentrated around Suharto's personal rule.

Having said this, the viability of Suharto's form of rule did ultimately depend on economic growth and development (Robison 1986: 105–130; MacIntyre 2000: 248–273). From 1969 onwards, the national five-year development programmes (REPELITA—Rencana Pembangunan Lima Tahun) formed major planks of an interventionist, export-oriented industrialization. This helped modernize the country's infrastructure and transform its economic production base. Yet, the rent-seeking behavior and financial base of Suharto's crony capitalism was heavily dependent on resource revenues, especially those generated by Pertamina, the state-owned oil and gas monopoly. In the 1970s and early 1980s, oil and gas exports defined Indonesia's political economy and, for a time at least, shielded it from market realities with oil prices spiraling following the Iranian revolution. By 1981, oil and gas accounted for 82 percent of all exports and 73 percent of government tax revenue (MacIntyre 2000: 248–273).

Suharto's control of this elaborate patronage machine ensured that virtually every important economic and political player, particularly the military, was dependent on some form of state patronage. This reliance on state patronage extended through Golkar across the archipelago with personal favours exchanged between state officials, business interests, and community elites. Suharto sat at the apex of not just a political structure but also "a system akin to business franchising." (McLeod 2000: 101). This allowed him "to bestow privileges on selected firms, so he effectively awarded franchises to other government officials at lower levels to act in a similar manner" (McLeod 2000: 101).

As a result, state actors had a hand in most aspects of economic activity. This government-led industrialization led to a pattern of economic growth beset by patrimonial rent-seeking and economic inequality. Throughout the 1980s, foreign investment fell due to restrictions on foreign investment and high subsidies given to state-owned companies. At the same time, the mutually beneficial economic joint ventures between military officers and major ethnic Chinese economic actors fueled resentment among indigenous economic interests (Robison 1986: 322–370). Patronage relationships formed between high-ranking state actors and ethnic Chinese entrepreneurs. Indonesian military men were the "masters" of politics and Chinese financial backers were the "masters" of capital (MacIntyre 2000: 248). Suharto's relationship with Mohamad 'Bob' Hasan (The Kian Seng) and Sudono Salim (Liem Sioe Liong) exemplified this *cukong* system of patronage.

Yet, as Herb Feith (1980) rightly pointed out, Suharto's "repressive developmentalism" relied too heavily on personal "cronyism" and resource revenues, a situation that brought about an incremental erosion of confidence in the banking sector in world markets, especially when the regime lost financial credibility in the wake of the 1997 Asian Financial Crisis. Suharto's regime was never able to match the more forceful policies and effective use of external development loans of say Thailand or South Korea. Richard Robison bluntly sums it up as an "entrenchment and centralization of authoritarian rule by the military, the appropriation of the state by its officials, and the exclusion of political parties from effective participation in the decision-making process" (1986: 105). To complete our anatomization of the Suharto regime, the following sections briefly outline the significance of the two main props of his patrimonial authority, namely, the Military and Golkar.

THE INDONESIAN MILITARY

Formerly known as ABRI (Angkatan Bersenjata Tentara Republik Indonesia—Armed Forces of the Republic of Indonesia), TNI (Tentara Nasional Indonesia—Indonesian National Defence Force) was one of the key players in maintaining this patrimonial corporatism. Even by the standards of bureaucratic authoritarianism, it occupied an unusual political role. This role traces back to armed resistance against colonial rule with the military securing a symbolic place in Indonesian iconography as the "guardian" of the Republic. It has been involved in the economic sector since the war of independence and the nationalization of Dutch colonial companies in the 1950s.

In the Sukarno era, military involvement in the economy became accepted practice in order to raise extrabudgetary revenue for operations. After 1958, its position as protector of the Republic's integrity took on a political character with greater involvement in economic and social development (Crouch 1979: 571–587). From 1958, a series of laws legitimized the military's dual function (*dwifungsi*) within the Indonesian Republic. First, Law No. 80/1958, and MPR Decree No. II/1960 (A/III/404/Sub/C) consolidated the military's power by guaranteeing it a fixed representation in Majelis Permusyawaratan Rakyat (MPR—People's Consultative Assembly), Dewan Perwakilan Rakyat (DPR—House of Representatives), and local parliaments. This effectively meant that the military was a functional group of the state.

Second, during the New Order era, Suharto further strengthened military influence across the political and economic landscape through Law No. 16/1969 and Law No. 5/1975 (Crouch 1979: 578–600). These laws officially recognized the military's dual function, and by the 1980s, the military was even involved in local development with its *masuk desa* programme. Suharto also gained support for his leadership in patrimonial fashion by engendering fear and distributing favours. He rewarded loyal military supporters and quelled dissent with appointments to civilian posts that offered prospects of material gain. Other officers were encouraged to go into business, with a promise of help from the administration whenever they needed licenses, credit, or contracts.

As a central prop of the New Order and protector of national integrity, it is hardly surprising that the military has retained a significant influence in the post-Suharto era. With only approximately 30 percent of the military's funding coming from the government, it has always been reluctant to have reform enforced upon it (Singh 2000: 184–216). Even with constitutional reform in 2002 and the formal removal of allocated seats in parliament in 2004, the military is still very much involved in the economy (Kingsbury 2003a: 188–220). Military-owned businesses operate in most areas of domestic investment and are involved in various joint ventures with foreign and Chinese partners.

The military's territorial structure also remains largely intact. This ensures that the KODAM (regional military commands), KOREM (sub-regional military commands), and KODIM (district military commands) have access to various types of revenue from fishing and logging to coffee production. Self-funding activity is further organized through a network of *yayasan* (charities similar to NGOs), not to mention the illegal levies, smuggling, and protection rackets (McCulloch 2003: 94–124). Although the military is no longer as politically powerful as it once was, its extensive economic weight means it is hard to ignore. This makes transforming its institutionally inculcated "culture of violence" a very challenging issue indeed (Colombijn and Linblad 2002).

GOLKAR

The other key player in Suharto's patrimonial/corporatist matrix was of course Golkar. Its prototype emerged from the Sukarno era in 1963 as the Joint Secretariat of Functional Groups. This ABRI-initiated prototype provided a framework for the military to mobilize civilian support in a united front against Partai Komunis Indonesia (PKI— Indonesian Communist Party). In 1965, when Suharto came to power, he along with General Ali Murtopo transformed these groupings into a state political machine for the New Order regime.

The "restructuring" of Indonesia's political system was central to establishing control over the machinery of patronage and allocation of resources. By 1971, Golkar, along with PDI and PPP, had become one of the three permissible state-licensed political parties. Yet, Golkar was able to ensure its electoral superiority over the other two parties with a combination patronage and a semi-monopoly on communications and funding (MacIntyre 2000: 248–273). In the elections on 3 July, 1971, Golkar secured 62.8 percent of the vote and won 227 of the 351 seats in the DPR. At its first congress in Surabaya in 1973, Golkar then amalgamated its constituent groups of military officers, cabinet ministers, and technocrats into a single powerful state machine. It developed a vast territorial reach at all levels of society with civil servants, government officials, administrators, and educators all expected to become cadre. This meant that throughout the New Order period, Golkar was able to supervise the allocation of resources and patronage across the archipelago. With its unrivaled access to state revenues, distinctive organizational structure, and a clearly recognizable symbolic identity, Golkar dominated the national and local legislatures. Institutionally speaking, both Golkar and the military functioned as operational mechanisms for Suharto's control over resources.

Their hegemonic presence allowed Suharto to weave a web of corruption through the executive, legislative, and judicial institutions of the Indonesian state. They allowed him to operationalize his patrimonial authority through a vast alliance of state officials, business interests, and community elites reaching all the way down the chain to the village level. Having said this, despite its territorial reach, Golkar actually lacked strong leadership because Suharto actively promoted factions (Tomsa 2008). This was all part of his divide-and-rule strategy that allowed him to shore up his authority. In fact, Suharto's highly centralized rule meant that Golkar ultimately turned into more of a personal political vehicle. He pressed it into service to mobilize public support for his policies and secure his reappointment by MPR, but, at the same time, he denied it any major policy formation role or strong programmatic platform. This means that Golkar's status as a leading political party in the post-Suharto era is not really based on the merits of strong programmatic initiatives but more by taking advantage of its hegemonic past.

CONCLUSION

As this chapter briefly demonstrates, reading multiple narratives into the contextual background of democratization is a useful step in understanding the strategies political actors adopt toward democratic opening. What it helps avoid is an overly voluntaristic interpretation of political action during democratization by contextualizing the agency involved. Similarly, identifying a process of multiple interlinking constraints and potentialities to political action provides a less structurally deterministic reading of the emerging pattern of democratic politics. By anatomizing major aspects of Indonesia's past, especially the New Order era, we can see it had certain ideational characteristics, that is, nationalism, a depoliticized Islam, centralized patrimonial authority, and a repressive developmentalism. In the aftermath of Suharto, these ideational and institutional characteristics did not simply disappear but rather constituted part of the terrain of Indonesia's democratization process. As a result, they are potentially implicit constraints depending on how political elites renegotiate them. As we shall see, the subsequent interplay between political renegotiation and these embedded institutional rigidities and culturally informed behavior patterns can have a significant impact on the democracy establishing itself. Indeed, the ambiguity inherent in Indonesia's postauthoritarian settlement arises in no small part from compromises enacted through the contestation and reinterpretation of these realities.

PART III

INDONESIAN DEMOCRATIZATION

CHAPTER 3

DEMOCRATIZATION AND
POLITIK ALIRAN

Everyone knows that different political cultures affect democratization in different ways. Yet, merely to state this raises complex issues of interpretation and meaning that we all struggle to grasp. For instance, regardless of type, regimes seek legitimacy for their authority and leadership. An authority and leadership that for Max Weber ([1924] 1962) fell into three archetypes, traditional, emotional, or rational-legal, and in reality, it is usually some mixture of all three. In Gramscian terms, however, this search for legitimacy involves nothing as obvious as direct coercion. Rather, it relies on an enmeshment of coercion and consent. A reciprocity between the former and latter facilitates the reproduction of a hegemonic form of political domination. As complicity is elicited through an ensemble of material, ideational, and discursive practices and strategies that order and sustain the configuration of power. Under the pervasive influence of a hegemonic bloc, the general populace internalize the ideas, values, and norms of the dominant social grouping thus legitimizing their rule by accepting as normal the formation of authority and leadership

(Gramsci 1971: 57). As Chapter 2 demonstrated, the discursive practices and strategies of both Sukarno and Suharto deployed traditional symbolic resources to systematically organize consent for the purposes of nation-state building and legitimacy.

Given these considerations, we can recognize that a transition from authoritarian rule may open the way for further democratic change, but preexisting structures, institutions, symbolic markers and discursive practices already inhabit the formation of new political space. They echo the polity's self-understanding and provide a range of resources and options for political decision-makers—who initiate change—to draw upon selectively. In effect, if established elites preside over a transition in an attempt to maintain their presence, then they utilize a metonymic assemblage of relevant symbolic markers and discursive practices that both tacitly or explicitly appeals to popular societal sentiments and engenders widespread consensus. This is both catalyst and break, as political actors negotiate not only the present but also the past. In other words, the grammar of political action that evolves to enact change simultaneously constrains it.

Of course, this is not to say things are predetermined, but rather material and ideational factors guide certain preferences and capacities. To appreciate the consensual aspects of this legitimization process during democratization, it is important to comprehend the political culture(s) of a society that embodies its own self-understanding. These are the values, beliefs, and attitudes shaping political formations within a society. We have to take into account not just economic structures but the ideational, cultural, and political conditions of existence in order to unravel the agency involved in enacting change.

The following chapter, therefore, considers the ability of established political elites in Indonesia to mobilize a modern heterogeneous society around a modified form of traditional cultural politics since 1998. First, by examining key aspects of political culture in Indonesia, it locates clues to how and why communal affinities or *aliran* (streams) reemerged in the political grammar of post-Suharto party politics. Second, through a comparison of the 1955 and 1999 elections, it considers the extent to which political parties are still socially rooted in *aliran* and what this means for the subsequent development of the Indonesian political system. Third, the chapter evaluates the analytical validity of *aliran* for explaining Indonesian politics, especially in the face of weakening cultural loyalties (*dealiranisasi*), corrosive "money politics," and the rise of presidential/charisma politics.

OUTLINING POLITICAL CULTURE IN INDONESIA

As Weber ([1924] 1962) pointed out, communities arrange themselves in a manner that distributes goods, tangible and intangible, symbolic and material. He viewed this distribution as unequal because it necessarily involved power relations whether between classes, status groups, or political parties. In these terms, subordinate individuals accept, or at least do not challenge, powerful and dominant individuals or groups. Having said this, the role political culture plays in this distribution of power is often misunderstood. It provides a form of orientation constituted by specific cultural traits (behaviors, beliefs, social relationships, and symbols) that shape particular societal structures and allow power to operate (Boas [1940] 1988: 4).

If we take this to mean the values and practices of contingent historical experience, political culture is an interpolated condition of self-understanding. Applying this to a basic sketch of political culture in Indonesia, Clifford Geertz (1960) developed a theory of primordial cultural attachment to explain social formations. While not wanting to represent Geertz's categorizations as definitive, historically at least, he did identify certain *aliran* (streams). For Geertz (1960: 37–41), these *aliran* reflected particular socioreligious-ethnocultural affinities and constituted major communal group identifications. In the context of political culture, this symbolized a specific form of self-understanding. In fact, during the 1970s, Donald Emmerson (1976) and Herb Feith and Lance Castles (1970) used them to explain Indonesian political development from the 1950s onwards in what was to become known as *politik aliran*, that is, mass-based political parties embedded within a specific cultural stream. The support for Indonesia's *aliran* political parties, as they emerged in the postcolonial context, had specific ethnocultural, religious, and political outlooks (Feith and Castles 1970: 5–7).

Other key theorists of Asian power and politics, Anderson (1972, 1990) and Lucian and Mary Pye (1985) further accommodated cultural understandings into their perceptions of political authority in Indonesian society. This helped shed light on the bureaucratic functionalism of the New Order. In the intervening years, however, various scholars rightly questioned the applicability of Geertzian symbolic ethnography as a framework for explaining Indonesian political developments, especially with increasing urbanization (Heryanto 1999; Philpott 2000; Nordholt 2003: 550–589). The argument was that more mobile and less traditionally attached middle classes had less affinity with traditional identifications. This is something considered in more detail in Chapter 5, but the main point is that politicized ethnicities are not solely located in some precolonial primordialism. Despite the validity of these criticisms, a modified version of *politik aliran* did reemerge in the uncertainty of the immediate post-Suharto period. There were marked similarities between the 1999 elections and the parliamentary elections in the 1950s as political elites utilized traditional categorizations to mobilize the populace. This strategy seemed to have a reassuring appeal, especially in rural areas.

Given the similarities, an important question to ask then is, what does the apparent reemergence of *politik aliran* mean for political development in Indonesia? To answer this, we need to outline some of the key characteristics of traditional *politik aliran*. The first thing to note is that the archipelago has a rich history of taking outside influences and adapting them to local traditions. It has been a geographical site of cross-cultural miscegenation since at least the fifth or sixth century. Alternately, Hinduism, Buddhism, Islam, and Christianity have all brought cultural influence to bear. Local traditional cultures adapted them to complement existing social patterns and power relations (Schiller and Schiller 1997). In modern-day context, one need only look at the fact that Jakarta celebrates Javanese, Chinese, and Islamic New Years to get the point.

Javanese, however, remain Indonesia's largest ethnic grouping. They have a strong bearing on politics and culture. Historically speaking, the Hindu caste system of social differentiation and stratification influenced Javanese society in terms of their being a status-conscious hierarchical mindset at play. As Koentjaraningrat (1985) points out, traditional Javanese elites liked to distinguish between lords (*gusti*) and subjects (*kawula*), especially in the agriculturally fertile lands of Central Java and more specifically around Yogyakarta and Solo. Having said this, this distinction was considerably less prevalent among coastal Javanese (*pesisir*) (Liddle 1996: 65). What is clear is that traditional

Javanese culture relied on specific power relations, that is, patron-client arrangements rather than strictly contractual relationships. This cultural specificity imbued Indonesia's developmental practices with a strong sense of paternalism and patronage.

To elaborate, for traditional Javanese culture, power was a zero-sum game; you had power or you did not. An increase in one's power could only come at the expense of loss of power for someone else. After a period of tumult, for instance, the *wahyu* (divine radiance) of the ruler would confirm accession to power. The leader demonstrated this by possessing several objects believed to hold supernatural powers. In his seminal work, *The Idea of Power in Javanese Culture*, Anderson drew attention to the influence of these traditional attitudes.

For Anderson (1972: 22),

[T]he core of the traditional polity has always been the ruler, who personifies the unity of society. This unity is in itself a central symbol of 'power', and it is this fact as much as the overt goals of the statist ideologies that helps to account for the obsessive concern with oneness which suffuses the political thinking of many contemporary Javanese.

This constellation of power requires a strong social identification with authority. There is no social contract in the modern liberal sense of rights, but there is an emphasis on responsibilities. Reciprocal respect forms the fulcrum on which this culture of obedience (*budaya petunjuk*) balances. Power is not a divine right of the ruler but achieved through the spiritual practice of putting community interests before his own (Anderson 1972: 22–27, 37–38). The ruler must display service mindedness (*jasa*) in order to maintain harmony. If not, the ruler will lose the support of the community. Those in power have a responsibility for their actions and can never demand obedience. If they resort to excessive coercion, this undermines their legitimacy and displays of generosity are a more traditional way of retaining support. Consequently, what we view as corrupt vote-buying in a Western sense, villagers often view it somewhat differently in Indonesia. Having said this, if villagers suspect *pamrih* (concealed self-interest), a ruler will lose support.

This takes on greater resonance if we apply it to interpret the demise of the New Order. Before 1998, there had been widespread suspicion about the levels of corruption, cronyism, and nepotism (*korupsi, kolusi, nepotisme*) under the auspices of Suharto and the New Order. There was an increasing atmosphere of dissatisfaction among the populace. Notwithstanding the economics of the situation, this is what eventually delegitimized Suharto's rule. In cultural terms, the exposure of Suharto's *pamrih* led to a loss of his *wahyu* in the eyes of the *wong cilik* (common people), resulting in his *lengser keprabon* (step-down from power).

Yet, given the archipelago's geography, it is hardly surprising that we find distinct variations to this Javanese model of power and legitimacy. For instance, Bataks, Dayaks, Acehnese, Minangkabaus, Malluccans, Minahasans, and Buginese, to name but a few, all have their own distinct cultural practices, beliefs, and societal structures (Bjork 2003: 184–216). In the precolonial era, Hindu social hierarchies had less influence on these socioethnic groupings than in Java. As a result, they display less elaborate social stratification and differentiation (Nordholt 2003: 550–589). Often situated on historical trading routes, there exist strong senses of territoriality and a seemingly more direct attitude between subordinate and superior. Certainly, if compared to the elaborate courtesies of high Javanese culture, their leaders are more accessible with less of a mystical aura about them.

Another important factor in the distinctive character of these regions is the influence of Islam. Different precolonial responses to encounters with Islam, over time, shaped distinct political cultures (Koentjaraningrat 1985: 94–95). Historically, in Java, there was no radical alteration of the existing political culture and institutional power relations, more an assimilation of Islam (Geertz 1960: 37). This syncretism is clearly visible in Javanese *abangan* (nominal Muslims) who blend animistic and Hindu beliefs and practices along with those of Islam. By contrast, East Javanese *santri*, with their complex religious boarding school system (*pesantren*), display considerably more piety. Outside Java, Islam has a strong influence in Aceh where it came to symbolize the golden age of the sixteenth century Iskandar Muda sultanate (Najib 1996: 40–47).

Historically at least, these various social aggregations provided cultural markers for three broadly identifiable cultural streams (*aliran*) in Indonesia, that is, *priyayi* (nobility—traditional bureaucratic elite), *abangan* (nominal Muslim), and *santri* (more orthodox Muslim). As such, they operated as cultural and political resources in the mobilization of political support that influenced the cultural politics of both the Sukarno and the Suharto eras. In fact, for political parties in the 1950s, sociocultural outlook was as important as ideological foundations. Indonesia's political leaders had to effectively represent specific ethnocultural groupings to secure support irrespective of class differentiation within that grouping (Anderson 1990: 68). Of course, as we shall see in the following chapters, in contemporary Indonesia, these Geertzian differentiations are no longer as clearly applicable or directly relevant, but they do still have some resonance in the polity's self-understanding.

To elaborate, in the immediate postcolonial context, influential Seberang intellectuals such as Sjahrir and a number of Western-educated Javanese intellectuals like Sumitro and Soedjatmoko adopted a socially democratic stance through Partai Sosialis Indonesia (PSI—Indonesian Socialist Party). PSI shared a close affinity with Masjumi, especially in relation to concern over communist ascendancy and central Javanese domination. While appealing to small number of urban bourgeoisie groupings, PSI performed poorly in the 1955 elections. On the other hand, two major political parties emerged with broad appeal to large numbers of *abangan,* especially rural peasants and labourers from the poorer more agricultural areas. Both the secular nationalist party, Partai Nasional Indonesia (PNI), and the communist party, Partai Komunis Indonesia (PKI), cut across class and gender lines. At the same time, they infused their political rhetoric with Javanese conceptions of power, leadership, and statecraft to symbolize, in attenuated form, the integrative harmony of mutual cooperation, *gotong royong* (Antlov 2000: 203–222). Both parties promoted a secular nation-state, because neither had any wish to see strict Shari'a law imposed (Barton and Fealy 1996: 65, 87). This appealed to and reflected *aliran kepercayaan,* the embodiment of *kebatinan* (Javanese syncretism). For its part, the PKI made inroads as an alternative to the PNI with crossover appeal to a large section of lower status *abangan* and rural Javanese *santri* in central and eastern Java. On a discursive level, they achieved this through a radicalization of traditional cultural understandings that infused them with the rhetoric of class and colonial oppression.

Ultimately, however, post-1965, Suharto sanctioned a brutal pogrom of persecution against the PKI and the political landscape witnessed the "disappearance" of an estimated 500,000 PKI sympathizers. Many PKI followers sought refuge from persecution by switching allegiance to PNI or Golkar. Capitalist development replaced the class struggle, with *priyayi* dominating the state apparatus and the dissemination of Javanese symbolism, cultural values, and power across the archipelago. In contrast, large concentrations of traditional Javanese *santri* Muslims identified with Nahdlatul Ulama (NU) especially in urban centers such as Yogyakarta, Surabaya, and Solo (formerly Surakata). NU promoted tolerance and maintained that Islam could indeed thrive under Pancasila. Consequently, this strong base of traditionalist *santri* had a better disposition to the centralized unitary state than modernist *santri* outside Java.

In the immediate postindependence era, Masjumi (the Council of Muslim Organizations) had given voice to the latter's concerns about a unitary and Javanese-dominated centralized state (Barton and Fealy 1996: 21). In 1956, NU supported Sukarno's continuing centralization of the government despite demands from regional commanders for more autonomy in the provinces. When Sukarno ignored these demands, rebellion flared and led Lieutenant Colonel Ahmad Hussein to declare the establishment of the Revolutionary Government of the Republic of Indonesia (PRRI) in Sumatra.

NU disassociated itself from the PRRI rebellion considering it damaging interests of Indonesia's Muslims. But prominent leaders of the independence struggle from both Masjumi and PSI, disillusioned by Javanese dominance, fled to Sumatra. Masjumi's Sjafruddin Prawiranegara became prime minister of the PRRI with help from PSI's Sjahrir. The rebellions and the PRRI proved short-lived as the Indonesian military moved in to crush them. Sukarno later banned Masjumi and PSI and jailed their leaders.

Post-Sukarno, Suharto's patrimonial corporatism further suppressed and co-opted *aliran* identification. Golkar (Golongkan Karya—Functional Groups), PDI (Partai

Demokrasi Indonesia—Indonesian Democratic Party), and PPP (Partai Persatuan Pembangunan—United Development Party) represented an ersatz form of *aliranisation* vis-à-vis New Order bureaucratic functionalism. Given this background, what does the strength of *politik aliran's* reemergence say about post-Suharto Indonesia? It certainly corresponds with a time of extreme financial uncertainty and substantial political change.

THE RE-EMERGENCE OF POLITIK ALIRAN?

In 1997, just before Suharto's downfall, Indonesia experienced a series of calamitous events. Huge forest fires broke on Sumatra and Kalimantan sending a pall of smoke across the region. Ethnic violence erupted in West Kalimantan between Dayaks and Madurese settlers, an estimated 1,000 people died in the riots. On the political front, expelled from the PPP in 1995, Sri Bintang Pamungkasis received a jail sentence of thirty-four months in 1996 for insulting the president. He was subsequently released pending appeal and later rearrested on subversion charges for founding a reformist political party. On the back of all these domestic issues, the Asian Financial Crisis (AFC) swept in with a catastrophic impact. The Indonesian rupiah began to fall in tandem with other regional currencies and soon went into free fall against world currencies (Basri 1999: 27–37).

Simultaneously, Indonesia experienced its worst drought in fifty years and the banking sector collapsed under a mountain of bad loans. With the rupiah nose-diving, inflation soared, and by late 1997, more than 80 percent of Indonesian companies borrowing from foreign banks and listed on the Jakarta Stock Exchange were technically bankrupt. By early 1998, rioting had broken out across the archipelago over food shortages and rising prices. The prices of oil, gas, and other commodity exports plummeted to such an extent that the per capita GDP fell by 13 percent.

On March 10, 1998, large student protests in Java and Ujung Pandang called for Suharto's overthrow. In response, Suharto tried to deflect public anger by blaming Chinese and global financial institutions for the crisis. As a result, angry mobs rioted in Glodok (the Chinese district of West Jakarta), killing 1000 ethnic Chinese. By April, riots had spread from Jakarta to Solo in central Java and Medan in northern Sumatra. Student protests turned violent as they clashed with police. The death of four Trisakti University students shocked many ordinary Indonesians. In this climate of violence, divisions appeared in the once-unified regime. ICMI (Ikatan Cendekiawan Muslim Indonesia— the Association of Muslim Intellectuals) demanded moderation and turned to B. J. Habibie instead (Raysid 2000: 151–156). It seemed the only way to avert further crisis was to remove Suharto from the heart of the body politic. By May 1998, Suharto's grip on power was gone amidst growing elite dissension and continuing mass protests. He duly stepped aside on May 21, 1998.

What these brief but dramatic events created was a crisis of uncertainty and legitimacy. The articulation of a stabilizing grammar of political action became an essential requirement to appeal to and reassure an unsettled Indonesian populace demanding change. In fact, the very atmosphere of uncertainty and change allowed leading political actors to capture the imagination of the general populace (King 2003: 139–165). A feat they achieved by reinvoking the past and appealing to half-remembered memories. This situation goes some way to explain the striking resemblances between the parliamentary elections in 1955 and the elections of 1999.

For instance, in 1955, four political parties representing the three major *aliran* took 77 percent of the vote. PNI led by Sukarno won 22 percent of the vote with 16 percent of the vote going to PKI. Both had appeal for *abangan* and non-Muslim voters. NU represented the interests of traditionalist Muslims with 18 percent of the vote and the modernist Islamic Masjumi took 21 percent. Two Christian parties, one Islamic party, and PSI drew another 9.5 percent of the total vote.

Similarly, in 1999, Partai Demokrasi Indonesia— Perjuangan (PDI-P, the Indonesian Democratic Party– Struggle) as the successor of Sukarno's PNI provided a vehicle for secular nationalists. PDI-P achieved the same 37 percent of vote in 1999 as the combined PNI/PKI vote in 1955. Significantly, PDI-P's vote outside Java also increased compared to the PNI's in 1955, most notably in Bali because of Megawati Sukarnoputri's connection to the island. Nonetheless, the regional spread of allegiance remained broadly similar between 1955 and 1999. Java remained a stronghold for secular nationalist and tradition- alist Muslim voters. Just like NU in 1955, Partai Kebangki- tan Bangsa (PKB—National Awakening Party) acquired its parliamentary seats overwhelmingly from Java. However, its vote outside Java shrank by more than half in 1999.

In contrast to PKB, modernist Islamic parties received most of their parliamentary seats from outside Java, espe- cially Sumatra and Sulawesi. The modernist Islamic parties PPP, Partai Amanat Nasional (PAN—National Mandate Party), Partai Bulan Bintang (PBB—Crescent Star Party), and Partai Keadilan (PK—Justice Party) combined polled 22 percent of the vote in 1999, similar to Masjumi's 24 percent in 1955.

Having said this, the major difference between 1955 and 1999 is clearly the presence of Golkar and absence of the PKI in 1999. This goes someway to explaining why mod- ernist Islamic parties were less successful in picking up the votes from their predecessor parties outside Java in 1999. Despite suffering a hemorrhage of support in the euphoria of *reformasi*, Golkar's institutional structure remained intact and ended up polling 21 percent. B. J. Habibie was able to rely on Golkar's Muslim factions to maintain allegiance from major *abangan* and *santri* constituencies (Antlov and Cederroth 2004: 111–137). With the exception of Aceh, a discredited and temporarily disorientated Golkar still managed to win much of the old Masjumi vote, especially in eastern Indonesia.

Despite these notable discrepancies, what the similarity between the elections of 1955 and 1999 show is that in a time of uncertainty people tend to incline toward the familiar. Similar voting patterns between the two elections suggested that significant electoral constituencies remained attached to traditional religious, regional, and social affiliations. Despite the greater number of political parties in 1999 than in 1955, PDI-P, PKB, PPP, and to some extent PAN appealed to the three major *aliran*. Top-level political actors managed events in 1999 by wrapping the promise of change in old loyalties. This reversion to old forms would have been familiar to someone from 1955 with the appeal to traditional identifications that had remained significant despite, or even because of, new realities.

If we take Golkar out of the equation for a moment, it is clear that the other three major political parties—PDI-P, PKB, and PPP—bet their party identity on an appeal to *aliran* or what they viewed as *priyayi-abangan*, traditional *santri*, and modernist *santri* constituencies respectively. This was no accident; it provided a particular lens to focus popular attention and tapped into a vaguely recognized reflection of cultural memory. In fact, the *piagam perjuangan* (fighting programs) of these parties contained minimal content. Rather than differentiated platforms of fiscal policy, political reform, or economic management, what they stood for in a time of uncertainty was the certainty of long established if anachronistic cultural orientations. From an electoral point of view, this effectively sidelined many of the activists behind the *reformasi* movement who were unable to compete with established political elites.

CONCLUSION

In certain instances, political change can be sudden, as it was in Indonesia. On the other hand, it seems that culture, while subject to adaptation, is resilient. What the Indonesian case highlights is that despite, or maybe because of, rapid change in 1999, the initial success of Indonesian political parties depended largely on their ability to reflect a cultural memory or at least a sense of it. In the uncertainty of the immediate post-Suharto era, however, this was more practical exigency than cultural necessity. Not only was *politik aliran* reassuringly familiar, but it provided an effective political resource to mobilize voters.

Having said this, although PDI-P flourished as the natural successor of PNI and a large social movement built up around it on the promise of change, it remained institutionally weak. Moreover, the Megawati Sukarnoputri presidency (2001–2004) may have brought relative political stability, but she failed to live up to the socioeconomic expectations of her *abangan* constituency. With a lack of structure and coordination, PDI-P subsequently hemorrhaged support in 2004. As a result, Golkar took the legislative elections with 128 of the 550 seats compared to 109 for PDI-P, a retreat from 153 in 1999. In fact, Golkar was able to reassert political influence more by default than on a resounding political platform. After years of distributing state patronage to a range of constituencies both secular and religious, its greater territorial reach exposed PDI-P failings. On the other hand, Golkar does have institutional weaknesses of its own. It lacks a strong programmatic platform and has made limited attempts to infuse its political values among its constituencies, both of which came back to haunt it in 2009.

Certainly, things are not exclusively a case of history repeating itself. Indonesia's socioeconomic makeup has changed radically with new urban social formations showing less attachment to *aliran* loyalties (*dealiranisasi*). The pull of *aliran* is no longer as strong for these urban dwellers, their attitudes tempered by a strong dose of mistrust about levels of corruption and self-interest within established political parties. This is something evidenced by the rise of Hidayat Nur Wahid's Partai Keadilan Sejahtera (PKS—Welfare/Justice Party, formerly Partai Keadilan) and, more significantly, Susilo Bambang Yudhoyono's (SBY) Partai Demokrat (PD—Democratic Party). Although ex-military, SBY was one of a number of reformist junior officers in the early 1990s that pushed Suharto to negotiate with the democratic opposition and implement democratic reforms. Coupled with an urbane style, he seems to offer something different from the past but with a sense of reassuring stability about it. In short, the populace like SBY. The following chapters further consider the emergence of new allegiances and their influence on developments in Indonesia's political system.

CHAPTER 4

DEMOCRATIZATION AND ISLAMIC POLITICS

In 1998, with a transition from authoritarian rule underway, Indonesia also experienced a burgeoning of political Islam. As the world's most populous Muslim nation, this raised concerns about mainstream Islamist ascendancy. Yet, a decade later, Indonesia seems to have accommodated a diversity of Islamic political expression. The following chapter considers the extent of this accommodation and the relationship between political Islam and democratization in Indonesia. It examines the material and ideational factors in play before, during, and after the transition to uncover important clues as to how and why Indonesia developed a broad range of political Islamic expression within a democratic framework.

HISTORICAL ISLAMIC IDENTIFICATION

To begin with, there needs to be some quick clarification. Contemporary political Islam should not to be confused with Islam as a religion. Instead, it refers to an ideological interaction between politics and religion in the broadest sense. Having said this, it is important to differentiate Indonesian political Islam from Islamism. The latter is specifically concerned with the modern politicization of Islamic cultural concepts and symbols in an orthodox manner for radical ends, that is, the establishment of an Islamic state, or at least an Islamic polity with observance of Shari'a law. On the other hand, although often used inaccurately and interchangeably with Islamism, political Islam in Indonesia encompasses a considerably more complex plurality of expression and representation.

This plurality traces back to Islam's long-established historical roots in Indonesia. Dating back to the fourteenth century, Islam first arrived on Indonesian shores via trading merchants from Persia and India. In fact, in amalgamation with *adat* (traditional customs), it plays a significant role in many of the archipelago's diverse cultural identities. The syncretism of its adoption means that Islam is notably diverse in its manner of expression and depth of commitment across Indonesia. For instance, on Java, there is a distinct difference, in terms of religiosity, between two major Islamic strands. Nominal Javanese Muslims, *abangan*, identify with an indigenized syncretic *Agami Jawi*, while stricter *santri* or *muslimin* practice *Agami Islam santri* and also adopt traditionalist or modernist outlooks. Agami Jawi is viewed as a more open and tolerant form of practice while the latter is seen as more puritan, closer in expression to Arabian orthodoxy.

Outside Java, places like Aceh in northern Sumatra and parts of the Moluccas and central Sulawesi observe strict Islamic practice. In fact, it would be fair to say that *khittah* (cultural-religious identification) across the archipelago is a key feature of the polity's language of self-understanding. One need only look at the size of Indonesia's two major socioreligious organizations to appreciate the influence of Islam in daily life. The traditionalist Sunni Islamic

Nahdlatul Ulama (NU—Awakening of Ulama) boasts in the region of 30–35 million members, while membership of the reformist Muhammadiyah (followers of Muhammad), which identifies with the Islamic legacy left by Masjumi (Council of Muslim Organisations), is approximately 29 million strong.

NATIONALISM, ISLAM, AND THE REPUBLIC

Having said this, throughout the colonial and postcolonial periods, an uneasy relationship formed between the modern Indonesian state and the polity's cultural-religious identification. Consequently, there is, on the one hand, historical acknowledgement of Islam but also a concomitant state-level containment of its political appeal (Hamayotsu 2002: 353–375).

To elaborate, as discussed earlier, during the struggle for independence, Islam developed three major political responses to and within the emerging national project. There was the traditionalist Sunni Islamic organization, NU, a modernist Islamic political party, Masjumi, and the militant Islamist movements, Darul Islam (DI—Abode of Islam) and Tentara Islam Indonesia (TII—Indonesian Islamic Army). DI and TII were revolutionary Islamic movements with similarities to the Islamic Brotherhood in Nasser's Egypt. They formed out of Islamic militias who opposed the Dutch in Java as part of the long anticolonial struggle for independence. In the immediate postindependence era, Masjumi was the prominent Islamic party and its leaders played major roles in the fledgling republic.

Yet, the new Republic under the secular nationalism of both Sukarno and Suharto frustrated the political ambitions of these organizations by imposing major restrictions on a politicized Islam. For instance, between 1948 and 1963,

Sukarno banned DI and TII. They carried on fighting for an Islamic State (NII—Negara Islam Indonesia) under the leadership of S. M. Kartosuwiryo, primarily in West Java, South Sulawesi, and Aceh. Their forces peaked in 1957 with an army estimated to be 13,000 strong. In 1962, DI and TII were eventually defeated after the Indonesian armed forces captured and executed Kartosuwiryo. Significantly, after 1949, Sukarno repositioned the significance of Islam in the national-political project by dropping the "Jakarta Charter" (which obligated Muslims to implement Islamic law) from the constitution. This left many stricter Muslims, particularly from outside Java, with the sense that the finalized constitution marginalized Islam and reinforced central Javanese dominance of the new republic. As if to reinforce this perception, Sukarno's subsequent quashing of the PRRI (Revolutionary Government of the Republic of Indonesia) rebellion in 1959 led to the prohibition and collapse of Masjumi.

Following the events of 1965, Suharto's Orde Baru (New Order) also went on to stymie political Islam's former influence by refusing Masjumi any sort of return. In fact, Suharto's overhaul of the electoral system in 1971 effectively de-Islamised Indonesia's state-level political structure. This allowed Golkar to dominate the electoral system after Suharto had forced the major Islamic organizations to come under the banner of one political party Partai Persatuan Pembangunan (PPP—the United Development Party). In practical terms, PPP was the only vehicle through which NU and Muhammadiyah could gain political representation.

Yet, despite Suharto's attempt to subsume the polity's Islamic identification to the diktats of New Order corporatism, it remained only partially successful (Barton 2002: 1–15). In reality, this marginalization of political Islam only precipitated greater civil society activity focusing on building a dynamic Islamic community based on education and social welfare. Rather than directly challenge for political power, reformists like Dawan Rahardjo, Djohan Effendi, and Nurcholish Madjid viewed Islamic development through social organizations as their new raison d'être. Their ideas on Islamic social and educational renewal emerged in close association with Himpunan Mahasiswa (HMI—Association of Muslim Students). They championed the building of Ikatan Cendekiawan Muslim Indonesia (ICMI—Association of Muslim Intellectuals). ICMI formed with Suharto's blessing. He saw it in terms of his own political advantage, as he was keen to court Islamic support to counter growing dissent from the military and prodemocracy activists. ICMI appealed to a younger generation of well-educated urban middle class who enjoyed increased access to strategic positions within business, government service, and academia.

By the 1990s, ICMI and Majelis Ulama Indonesia (MUI—Council of Indonesian Ulama) helped facilitate the launch of Islamic news media, *Republika* and *Ummat,* together with the Muslim educational foundation, *yayasan* Abdi Bangsa. This indirectly helped to restore Islamic issues onto the political agenda. Interestingly, keen to court Islamic support as a counter to growing prodemocracy sentiment and rumbling military dissent, Suharto even began to encourage such developments. Indeed, it was politically advantageous to tolerate Islamic political activism and promote pro-Islamic officers in the army (Kadir 1999: 22–24). Major figureheads within ICMI such as Amien Rais, Sri Bintang Pamungkas, Eggy Sudjanan, Din Syamsudin, and Adi Sasono symbolized this growing Islamic political influence. From Suharto's perspective, the likes of ICMI countered organizations beyond his direct control such as Muhammadiyah and NU. Although this shored up his friable authority, the strategy would eventually backfire in the wake of the 1997 financial crisis.

DEMOCRATIC TRANSITION AND POLITICAL ISLAM

Evidently, during a transition from authoritarian rule, an intricate interplay takes place between a polity's grammar of self-understanding and the impetus for change. Political actors must selectively utilize this grammar of self-understanding to speak to the disarticulated political space of authoritarian breakdown. Belief systems, social relationship patterns, and a mass audience accustomed to viewing politics through extant symbolic lenses, therefore, play important roles in the success, or otherwise, of the process.

To elaborate, by 1998 pro-Islamic figures within ICMI, like Din Syamsudin, began to question Suharto's authority. With the help of major donations from Saudi Arabia and Kuwait, Syamsudin had been instrumental in bolstering the orthodox Dewan Dakwah Islamiyah Indonesia (DDII—Islamic Propagation Council of Indonesia) and Komite Indonesia Untuk Solidaritas dengan Dunia Islam (KISDI—Indonesian Committee for Solidarity of the Islamic World). Subsequently, with Suharto's grip on power loosening in the face of economic meltdown and pressure for *reformasi*, orthodox sections in the green (Islamic) wing of the military began shifting their support to DDII and KISDI. Given the turbulent political climate, the DDII-KISDI-military alliance eventually abandoned Suharto, as they saw him as a liability to the interests of Islam.

Notwithstanding this alliance, an overriding sense of tolerance and the diversity of Islamic expression made the possibility of a united orthodox Islamist front distinctly remote. In fact, key figures in the *reformasi* struggle, the prominent Islamic leaders, Abdurrahman Wahid and Amien Rais and the likes of the late Nurcholish Madjid, were instrumental in maintaining public support for democratic change (Azra 2000: 309–318). All three continually emphasized the compatibility of Islam with democracy. In the turmoil of 1998, this was a crucially important stance to take, as many Muslim activists were on the front line of the rallies against Suharto's regime. By doing so, they effectively prevented calls for the creation of an Islamic state gaining any sort of credence.

Even with Suharto stepping aside, Wahid continued to remain wary of NU's political return, viewing this as potentially damaging to its social mission. He preferred to stress moderation and support for Pancasila as the way to promote Islam in the national interest. Eventually, however, pressure from NU's *kyai* (religious leaders) persuaded Wahid to reconsider and form Partai Kebangkitan Bangsa (PKB—National Awakening Party). Likewise, tensions between Wahid and his uncle, Yusuf Hasyim, and brother, Salahuddin Wahid, led them to the form Partai Kebangkitan Ummat (PKU—Muslim Nation Awakening Party).

By late 1998, the prospect of a single Islamic political voice was remote with forty out of the eighty political parties to varying degrees (Kadir 1999: 21–44). Although this number decreased by election time in 1999, twenty Islamic parties remained eligible. Most significantly, Amien Rais of Muhammadiyah formed the populist Partai Amanat Rakyat (PAN—National Mandate Party) after unsuccessfully seeking alliance with, among others, PPP. Yusril Ihza Mahendra took up the leadership of Partai Bulan Bintang (PBB—Crescent and Star Party). Other parties with stricter Islamic agendas included, Partai Keadilan (PK—Justice Party), Partai Ummat Islam (PUI—Muslim Believers' Party), and Partai

Masjumi Baru (PMB—New Masjumi Party). In addition, the orthodox Islamic movements, KISDI, DDII, Kesatuan Aksi Mahasiswa Muslim Indonesia (KAMMI—United Action of Indonesian Muslim Students), and the Asosiasi Partai-Partai Islam (APPI—Association of Islamic Parties) formed strong links with PK and PBB. DDII and KISDI also remained supportive of B. J. Habibie in an attempt to offset Muslim support for the secular-nationalist Megawati Sukarnoputri and Partai Demokrasi Indonesia—Perjuangan (PDI-P—the Indonesian Democratic Party–Struggle). Similarly, MUI and Kongres Umat Islam Indonesia (KUII—Congress of the Indonesian Islamic Community) urged Muslims to vote for an Islamic party. All these organizations exerted considerable political pressure that the next president be pro-Muslim.

They played no small part in Wahid becoming president despite Megawati Sukarnoputri's PDI-P taking 37.4 percent of the vote and 153 seats in parliament compared to Wahid's PKB taking 12.6 percent of the vote and 51 seats in parliament. Notwithstanding increased Islamic influence, the Wahid presidency failed to survive. In fact, the confusion surrounding his presidency embodied transition uncertainty. He was simply unable to hold a broad coalition of competing interests together. In fact, factional infighting and turmoil blighted the Wahid period with shifting alliances maneuvering to secure positions of influence (Barton 2001: 312–317; Mietzner 2001: 29–44). Wahid did little to improve the situation by dismissing several cabinet ministers. He also marginalized several top-ranking generals and caused consternation in conservative military ranks through his willingness to negotiate with separatists in Aceh.

This created an uneasy relationship between government and parliament that led to gridlock. Conservative political and military elites began to perceive Wahid as a threat to the status quo. Elite dissent resulted in a power struggle that saw Wahid accused of incompetence in running the executive and implicated in the "Bulogate" and "Bruneigate" corruption scandals, all of which culminated in his impeachment in mid-2001. The unforeseen consequence of this, however, was that it left Islamic groups with the unpalatable option of supporting Megawati Sukarnoputri, the then vice president, as the next president.

Political machinations aside, a significant outcome of this expansion in the post-Suharto party-system is the introduction of political players capable of appealing to major Muslim constituencies, especially PKB, PAN, PBB, and PKS (Partai Keadilan Sejahtera—Welfare/Justice Party, formerly PK). Similar to Malaysia, Islamic revival among Indonesian middle classes has no doubt helped bolster their political appeal. In fact, the political uncertainty and economic instability of the immediate post-Suharto era witnessed a noticeable retreat by conservative-minded urban middle classes into stricter forms of Muslim identity politics.

As a result, the likes of Hidayat Nur Wahid's PKS and Yusril Izha Mahendra's PBB benefited. The rise of PKS, in particular, coincided with the unraveling of the Megawati presidency. Its vote rose significantly from 1.5 percent in 1999 to 7.4 percent in 2004. Having said this, a more realistic explanation of PKS's electoral appeal in Jakarta and on university campuses is its newness and relatively untainted image. A younger, more conservative generation of urban Muslims support PKS because it comes across as a "clean" Islamic party. Much of its electoral success in 2004 was down to an anticorruption rather than a pro-Shari'a platform. Indeed, the fact that all the Islamic parties combined polled less than 42 percent of the vote in 1999 and there was no significant increase in 2004 reinforces this point. Nonetheless, what the reemergence of political Islam has done is introduce much needed electoral competition into the system. This new challenge means that established parties such as Golkar and PPP must adapt accordingly if they are to keep their pro-Islamic factions onside.

MILITANT ISLAMIST GROUPS

Fortunately, in the ten years since the transition, concern over mainstream Islamist ascendancy has proven largely unfounded. Of more concern, however, is a proliferation of Islamist paramilitary groups. They include Laskar Pembela Islam (LPI—Defenders of Islam Army), which operates as the paramilitary wing of the hard-line Front Pembela Islam (FPI—Islamic Defender Front). There is also Laskar Jihad (LJ—Army of Jihad), a militant offshoot of Forum Komunikasi Ahlus Sunnah wal-Jama'ah (FKAWJ—Forum for Followers of the Sunna and the Community of the Prophet). Similarly, the paramilitary Laskar Mujahidin Indonesia (LMI—Indonesian Mujahidin Militia) is an offshoot of Majelis Mujahidin Indonesia (MMI—Indonesian Mujahidin Assembly) and both Jemaah Islamiyah (JI—Islamic Community) and Angkatan Mujahideen Islam Nusantara (AMIN—Nusantara Islamic Jihad Forces) emerged from the extremist DI.

This contemporary proliferation has significant antecedents with roots back to the Islamic militias who fought in the anticolonial struggle for independence, namely, DI and TII. As mentioned earlier in the chapter, after Sukarno banned both DI and TII, their followers continued to fight for an Islamic State between 1948 and 1963, primarily in West Java, South Sulawesi, and Aceh.

A significant difference between now and then, however, is the arrival of *hadrami* (Indonesians of Middle Eastern descent) who have provided influential tutelage. Many of the latter fought with the *mujahidin* in Afghanistan in the late 1980s and later moved to Indonesia, bringing with them years of combat experience. In fact, some of the current militant groups have pan-Islamic ambitions. For instance, under the spiritual guidance of radical Muslim cleric and leader of MMI, Abu Bakar Bashir, JI's aim is to build *Darul Islam nusantara* (an archipelagic Islamic state). This would involve replacing the secular governments of Indonesia, Malaysia, and Singapore with an Islamic theocracy. JI (an organization not banned in Indonesia) has links to al-Qaeda networks across Southeast Asia and operates more like a regional franchise. In fact, its capacity to conduct Jihadist operations implicate it in the 2002 bombings in Bali and Sulawesi, the 2003 Jakarta Marriott Hotel bombing, and the 2004 suicide bombings at the Australian Embassy in Jakarta. The most recent bombings in Jakarta in 2009 are, however, more likely to have been masterminded by a splinter group from JI.

Somewhat differently, LPI and LJ both publicly deny any links with al-Qaeda, claiming instead to focus on domestic issues, something that allegedly explains their involvement in internecine conflict. LJ, in particular, views itself as the protector of Muslims on the Molucco islands where it is very active. Despite denials, suspicion persists that both LPI and LJ enjoy indirect support from orthodox Islamic organizations, namely, DDII and KISDI in addition to sympathetic "green" factions in the armed forces.

Of course, in domestic terms, given Indonesia's recent authoritarian past, dealing with this militant threat is a sensitive political issue. The government does not wish to polarize the moderate Islamic majority or impinge on newly acquired democratic freedoms. With the notorious 1963 *UU anti-subversi* (antisubversion laws) still fresh in the memories of many Indonesians, there is no political capital in resurrecting the specter of military repression.

Having said this, on October 18, 2002, parliament issued the antiterrorism Decree No. 1 and No. 2/2002 after gaining widespread public support. This move gave Badan Intelijens negara (BIN—the National Intelligence Agency) greater powers to identify terrorist suspects. Susilo Bambang Yudhoyono's government is also now actively cooperating with Malaysia, Singapore, the Philippines, and Australia to combat terrorism across Southeast Asia. Significantly, despite the extreme threat posed by militant Islamist groups, especially after the recent Jakarta bombings in 2009, mainstream Indonesian society continues to marginalize them.

CONCLUSION

While Islamist political parties do exist, simple dichotomies appear ill-suited to Indonesia. The majority of Islamic involvement in electoral politics remains of a moderate kind and very far from being associated with the institution of an Islamist state. In fact, the 2004 and 2009 election results suggest that this moderation is the predominant electoral norm, with a majority of Muslims more interested in a democratic nation-state. What is evident, though, is that Islamic political parties are now more prevalent than at any time in the past, a reassertion that has introduced unforeseen competition into the party system. This is something that not only influences the grammar of Indonesia politics but also challenges the appeal of established political elites. As pro-Islamic political players firmly establish themselves, there is no reason to assume that developments in Indonesian democracy will necessarily reflect Western norms. With Islam representing an important part of Indonesia's democratic evolution, it will be interesting to see how the political system continues to adapt.

CHAPTER 5

DEMOCRATIZATION AND
THE MIDDLE CLASSES

In an ideal world, if not always in practice, democracy provides a system of governance to manage conflict politically, translate public will into policy, and distribute resources effectively.

It may be a goal of the development process, but this is where things get tricky. Chapter 1 established how our assumptions about development affect our views on how a political system democratizes and the components that it needs to do so effectively. It also showed that our causal narratives of democratic change continually stumble on the ambiguity of democratic experience.

To quickly recap, a key assumption of the modernization school is that the rise of an articulate urban middle class provides, if not the engine, at least a commitment to democratic change. This is because in the Barrington Moore (1966) sense of "no bourgeoisie, no democracy," they correspond with changing social identities and aspirations for more avenues of expression. Such a situation leads to growing demands for political representation and a greater legal-rational orientation in business. In fact, from this perspective, you could say that Indonesia's transition was possible due to compositional change in urban social structures. The economic growth and information technology revolution of the late 1980s and early 1990s transformed metropolitan Jakarta and with it attitudes and perceptions toward democratic change.

Somewhat differently, Adam Przeworski and Fernando Limongi (1993: 51–70; 1997: 155–183) also argue that the per capita GDP income of a country can undermine the sustainability of further democratic consolidation if it falls below US$2,500. For instance, four Third Wave democratizations with a per capita GDP of under US$1,000 had authoritarian regressions—India in 1975, Nigeria in 1984, Sudan in 1989, and Pakistan in 1990. Out of the twelve Third Wave democratizations with per capita GDP under US$2,500, five failed. And the only Third Wave democracy with a per capita GDP above US$2,500 to fail, Peru, had incomes only slightly above the threshold and suffered significant economic decline.

Unfortunately, what any of this fails to tell us either way is whether the rise in income level a priori creates a new middle class critical of the incumbent regime or one heavily dependent on it. Evidence suggests that the Asian middle classes have played a somewhat ambiguous role when it comes to democratization (Rodan 1996: 1–28, 40–71). This chapter sets out to test the strength of the latter claim against the key assumptions of the modernization school. First, by examining the contingent emergence of Indonesia's middle classes in the New Order era, it uncovers important clues to their politically ambiguous role. Second, it considers the extent to which established political elites are able to adapt to new sociopolitical aspirations and the changing role of Indonesia's middle classes.

Suharto's New Order and the Making of the Middle Classes

In analytic terms, translating Western-derived concepts of social structure, status, and power to non-Western contexts can be fraught with problems. Indonesia, for instance, is of a mosaic of economic interests, ethnic identifications, and income levels (Dick 1985: 71–92). One of the first things you notice about Indonesian middle classes is the lack of a particularly strong or coherent political identity. What differentiates them for more communitarian-minded sections of society is not exclusively the level of consumption but the way they go about it. More patterns of consumption oriented toward individual households than collective political demands. This apparent lack of cohesion challenges some of our assumptions about democratic change—in particular, Moore's (1966) thesis about democracy being the political outcome, in particular countries, of gradual economic development and the rise of a strong and vocal bourgeoisie who demand greater influence and participation in the political system.

In fact, it would seem that Moore's student Theda Skocpol (1979) is more apropos to Indonesia in terms of development. For Skocpol, the state was such a major social and political agent that it operated as an independent actor within society and partially autonomous from other interests. Applying this perspective, one could represent Indonesia as, essentially, a state "overdeveloped" in relation to an "underdeveloped" class structure. Moreover, as Sritua Arief and Adi Sasono (1973) note, Dutch colonialism played an instrumental role in marginalizing indigenous merchants in favor of ethnic Chinese and foreign bourgeoisie. Consequently, an asymmetrical relationship developed between the Indonesian state and a weak and dependent domestic bourgeoisie that provided the basis for state dominance over civil society. In the aftermath of independence, the state enjoyed relative autonomy but at the same time found itself trapped within a structure of peripheral capitalism (Alavi et al. 1982). This meant a type of development wedded to the demands of international capital.

Indonesia was internally dependent on the export of raw materials but externally dependent upon international markets and overseas finance. Even as domestic consumption rose, the domestic economy remained highly reliant on New Order largesse and vulnerable to international market fluctuations. Significantly, Sino-Indonesian business groups and foreign capital may have dominated an expanding private sector, but they were far from able to convert their economic strength into corresponding political influence and felt obliged to seek the protection of *pribumi* patrons. This meant that a strong middle class, with an independently motivated domestic business stratum (bourgeoisie) at its core, struggled to emerge under Suharto's New Order. Instead, a relatively weak domestic bourgeoisie swapped demands against state power for the stability of authoritarian corporatism.

Having said this, despite uneven regional distribution and the concentrated nature of economic power and influence, New Order development programmes did bring substantial gains for a growing middle class (Hill 1996: 229–235). In Indonesia, as in Thailand and Malaysia, aligned to a combination of both financial globalization and the regionalization of production, urban middle classes emerged within a generation. This new generation could "be counted among the winners" of Suharto's corporatist authoritarianism (Dick 1985: 87).

To give a brief sketch of the economic changes, inflation came down from 600 percent in 1965–1966 to 10 percent in 1969, and the Indonesian economy grew by 7.7 percent annually from 1971 to 1981. Increases in the price of oil between 1974 and 1979 underpinned the growth. This contributed massively to export earnings and government revenue that led to an impressive rise in real income per capita with the middle classes being substantial beneficiaries (MacIntyre 1991). Growth slowed to 4 percent in 1982–1986, but Suharto managed to avert the mounting threat to growth posed by drops in the price of oil by reorientating the economy from oil to nonoil exports. This helped further modernize the country's infrastructure and transform its economic production base to a manufacturing-led one. However, it did necessitate huge development loans and foreign investment.

The post–Plaza Accord boom years of 1987–1995 brought another impressive rise in real income per capita; by 1994, Indonesia's GNP per capita was US$790. Financial liberalization opened the floodgates for global financial capital, and foreign direct investment (FDI) in the late 1980s led by Japan, Korea, Taiwan, and overseas Chinese helped change Indonesia's socioeconomic profile. Industrial and new town development transformed suburban Jakarta with exploding population growth in places like Botabek, Bogor, Tangerang, and Bekasi. As a result, in Jakarta alone, the middle-class demographic increased from an estimated 400,000 in 1980 to 810,000 by 1995. The fast-expansion of the private sector led to a more complex economic base with a relatively small but vibrant middle-class stratum (Mackie 1990: 96). Total banking assets expanded from 63 trillion rupiah in 1983 to 484 trillion in 1992 with the number of banks increasing from 91 in 1988 to 214 in 1993 (MacIntyre 2000: 250–256). Real estate prices soared in Jakarta's central business district (the Golden Triangle) as it reverberated in a clamor of fast cars, shopping malls, and fancy restaurants.

This brought with it new bargaining relationships between the state and some industry groups, especially in the insurance, textile, and pharmaceutical sectors. In the early 1990s, for instance, Suharto's short-lived exercise in *keterbukaan* (greater political openness) was an attempt to respond to growing demands. New Order corporatism needed to show a more inclusive face. Suharto briefly permitted a more independent press. The likes of *Tempo*, *Editor*, and *Detik* enjoyed unprecedented press freedom before the regime eventually withdrew their publishing licences. During this short-lived hiatus, organizations promoting middle-class interests also proliferated, for example, the Self-Reliant Community Development Institute (LSM), the Institution for Promoting Self-Reliant Community Development (LPM), the Legal Aid Institute (LBH), the Democracy Forum and the Institute for the Defence of Human Rights. Their emergence gave added voice to middle-class aspirations.

These minor developments gave the impression of a more united middle-class assertiveness, but appearances can be deceptive, especially in Indonesia. There were many divisions, especially between Sino-Indonesians (ethnic Chinese) and *pribumi* (ethnic Indonesians), and not much common ground between those dependent on Suharto's family and crony businesses and more independent-minded professionals and executives. This created a friction across the public-private sector divide (Heryanto 1999: 159–187). It meant that there was, in reality, a lack of independent critical mass to overcome Suharto, even with tangible threats to middle-class interests. One of the main reasons behind this was the continuing dependence of a large number of the new middle class on political and economic patronage.

A web of patronage controlled the relationships between the state bureaucracy, entrepreneurs, and business classes.

What this did was effectively tie Sino-Indonesian and *pribumi* conglomerates to the regime (MacIntyre 2000: 248). In fact, the New Order can be seen as, "a self-perpetuating patronage system from top to bottom, rewarding those who [are] in it and penalising all those who are excluded" (MacIntyre 1991: 45). Those who were "in" had little interest or ability to challenge the system. The middle classes were most definitely "in" and displayed a political ambivalence toward overturning the cozy economic status quo. The comforting embrace of the patronage system made them hesitant to sacrifice things for political change.

THE MIDDLE-CLASS EFFECT ON POST-SUHARTO POLITICS

At the lower levels of Indonesian society, however, development under an obstructive state of corporatism meant disempowerment not empowerment (Liddle 1992: 17–18). The middle classes may have been politically ambivalent, but *kampung* (urban slum) dwellers were impoverished and disaffected. All they needed was a spark and the Asian Financial Crisis (AFC) of 1997 duly provided one.

By the fall of 1997, the banking sector, which had already been in trouble under the weight of mounting bad loans, went into a systemic crisis with sixteen banks closing. The near collapse of the Indonesian banking system crippled state finances. Government debt rose to an estimated 92 percent of GDP, the servicing of which sucked revenues dry. This brought domestic and international investor confidence to an all-time low. As the full impact hit, prices shot up and food became scarcer. Chaos ensued as the urban poor began to riot. In the course of 1998, buoyed by vocal student protests, the momentum for change swelled with explicit criticism coming through a more confident media.

Suharto's attempts to sidestep IMF guidelines further undermined his credibility. The populace began to clearly recognize that the interests of his family and cronies took precedence over the interests of the nation. Consequently, middle-class loyalty to Suharto began to look increasingly conditional. This was because Suharto's hold over them had to a large extent always rested implicitly on his ability to provide economic benefits. He well knew the viability of his patrimonial rule depended on the continuing growth of the economy. An opposing logic he could no longer sustain. In fact, despite their somewhat marginal role in the actual transition itself, the middle classes have now gone on to play a much more significant role in the post-Suharto era. For instance, although established political elites exploited traditional geographical ethnic and cultural identities in the run-up to the 1999 elections, the new middle classes have markedly different outlooks on the loyalties of old. Urban development and better transportation facilities have brought significant one-way geographical mobility to large metropolitan centers, especially Jakarta. In this era of greater social mobility and increased political competition, overreliance on *politik aliran* by established political elites is in danger of backfiring.

The elections of 1999 may have relied on a top-down mobilization around old perspectives and loyalties and established party organization, but Indonesia's middle classes also displayed greater indifference toward traditional attachments than in the past. Their numbers are growing fast. Average income per capita, for example, rose to US$1,946 in 2007 from less than US$1,000 in 2003. If average income per capita reaches say US$2,400, then the top 10 percent of the population, which is approximately 22.5 million, will earn around US$7,000 per capita (Harinowo 2008). This educated and more politically conscious stratum is seeking parties with modern images and clear programmatic platforms. With these social transformations taking place, a party system organized along *aliran* lines may no longer be up to the task. Indonesia, it seems, is undergoing, for want of a better phrase, a form of urban *dealiranisi*.

To elaborate, the main political beneficiaries of Suharto's downfall were PDI-P and PKB. In the confused run-up to the 1999 election, both parties were able to consolidate their support by appealing to traditional *aliran*. For instance, Megawati Sukarnoputri, with her direct and nostalgic link to Sukarno, represented a broadly *abangan aliran*, Abdurrahman Wahid and Amien Rais, a broadly *santri aliran*. Golkar (Golongan Karya—Functional Groups), on the other hand, remained discredited and pretty much in disarray. Akbar Tanjung's defeat of Edi Sudradjat (former Defence Minister and Armed Forces Commander) for the leadership of Golkar had led to fragmentation. Former Army Chief of Staff Hartono went on to form *Partai Karya Peduli Bangsa* (PKPB—Concern for the Nation Party) and Sudradjat established Partai Keadilan dan Persatuan Indonesia (PKPI—Indonesian Justice and Unity Party). In uncertain times, these latter options had little appeal compared to the modified but more familiar *politik aliran* of Partai Demokrasi Indonesia—Perjuangan (PDI-P—the Indonesian Democratic Party–Struggle) and Partai Kebangkitan Bangsa (PKB—National Awakening Party). The middle classes voted accordingly.

On the other hand, they also had high expectations, and the conditionality of their support became increasingly apparent. As first, the controversial Wahid presidency and then the stagnation of the Megawati presidency failed to live up to expectations. Between 1999 and 2004, social cleavages and economic issues took on greater importance. As a result, political parties had to become more competitive to attract swing voters. They could no longer simply rely on bloc cultural votes, because their political performance was under increased scrutiny, especially in urban areas. Since the 1999 election, PDI-P has simply failed to consolidate its huge popular appeal. By 2004, it paid the ultimate electoral price for unfulfilled expectations and underperformance. With Donald K. Emmerson (2004: 94–108) tagging it "a year of voting dangerously," PDI-P's inability to counter Golkar hegemony and a lack of *aliran* loyalty among its middle-class constituencies saw them hemorrhage votes in 2004.

In fact, Golkar's victory in those elections exposed the limitations of *politik aliran* as an organizing principle of Indonesia's new party system. After going to the polls three times in the space of five months, Golkar reemerged as a dominant party organization in the new democratic system almost by default. It may have lost substantial support in Java to PDI-P and PKB, but with a distinctive organizational structure, well-established patronage networks, and symbolic identity, it largely maintained its 1999 vote in 2004. This may have been down to a bit of "voter fatigue," but the ability of Golkar to reinvent itself as a regionalist party with crosscutting appeal also paid dividends, especially in places like Sulawesi.

Certainly, compared to its rivals, Golkar's better institutionalization in terms of territorial reach and reification gives it an advantage, but there are flaws. A lack of charismatic leadership, compromised decisional autonomy, weak value infusion among its constituencies, and complacency in the recruitment of party cadre point to electoral weakness if challenged (Tomsa 2008). For Golkar to rely simply on other parties not improving may be a grave mistake. In fact, Susilo Bambang Yudhoyono's (SBY) Partai Demokrat (PD—Democratic Party) has recently taken advantage of this complacency. PD, combined with SBY's image as a *ksatria piningit* (hidden knight), offers a new style of notably demilitarised conservative politics that feels different from the past. This notably appeals to a middle-class demographic that seems to need reassurance. The 2009 legislative election victory for PD seems to reinforce the point.

CONCLUSION

Electoral trends in Indonesia suggest that the middle classes are exerting more influence but not without contradictory political consequences. On the one hand, there is support for openness and accountability in government, but on the other, they fear uncertainty and instability. Similarly, they favour new style politicians with media appeal but show little interest in anything more progressive. In short, they like greater choice but prefer order and stability. This may go some way to explain the rise of PD and PKS. PKS for one represents a break from the old politics but at the same time also offers a reassuringly conservative form of moral politics. PD reflects a newer, more urbane style of politics, but at the same time, SBY provides a sense of patrimonial stability, especially for former business cronies of Suharto who have been quick to ally themselves with PD.

In fact, the formula has proved so successful that it carried SBY and PD all the way to the wining post in the 2009 legislative election. PD took huge bites out of both the Golkar and PDI-P vote with 20.85 percent of the vote. This is up a staggering 13.35 percent from 2004. PD now has 148 seats in the DPR, up 91from 2004, compared to the 108 and 93 for Golkar and PDI-P, a fall of 20 and 16 seats respectively. What this indicates is that if older parties want to remain competitive, they will have to appeal to the new composition of Indonesian society rather than simply relying on old loyalties.

CHAPTER 6

Democratization and the Party System

Any breakdown of authoritarian rule is undoubtedly a positive development, but that is really just the beginning. One of the most important steps is to institute an effective party system capable of contesting the right to exercise legitimate control over public power and state apparatus. As the democratization literature suggests, this can provide a platform to promote broader norms of political behaviour and democratic consolidation (Linz and Stepan 1996). The actual process, however, is anything but smooth. There is necessarily a trade-off between popular political demands and pragmatic political choices as elite and popular forces interact in circumstances not of their own choosing. In dialectical terms, the negotiation of compromise generates some rather paradoxical and unexpected systemic outcomes (Munck 1993: 491; Bermeo 1997: 311). The following chapter considers why and how Indonesia's postauthoritarian party system looks the way it does.

To elaborate, in Indonesia, given the depoliticization of the New Order era, translating popular demand into effective representational capacity was always going to be a difficult proposition. In hindsight, Suharto's step down and the initial dynamics of reform conform more to an elite-dominated transition or what Huntington (1991: 114–118) has termed "transplacement." This is a situation where pressure from below generates a reform-from-within dynamic, something that allows moderate opposition to emerge through cracks in the old regime's previously united front but stops someway short of wholesale reform. In Indonesia, elite cohesion, although punctured, did not simply disintegrate in the face of external pressure. In fact, notwithstanding the catalyst of mass protests, negotiations between incumbent elites and moderate opposition figures effectively excluded protest activists.

Obviously, the students wanted to oust Suharto. At the same time, leading figures in a moderate opposition rebuffed their attempts to form a united front for change (Lane 1999). Protests may have led to Suharto's downfall, but crucially, they lacked the political organization to sustain pressure for radical reform. Rather, the "Ciganjur Four," consisting of Abdurrahman Wahid of NU, Megawati Sukarnoputri of PDI-P, Amien Rais of Muhammadiyah, and Hamengkubuwono X, the Sultan of Yogyakarta, took advantage of pressure from the students and schisms in the old regime to step onto the political stage. Regime figures like B. J. Habibie, and, to a lesser extent, General Wiranto, were willing to make concessions in the hope of securing a top-down guided democratization. Pragmatism and distinct fear of grassroot insurrection seemed the major motivating factors. Significantly, with B. J. Habibie's ascendancy to the presidency and interest from the middle classes, international media outlets, and diplomatic circles waning, protest demands began to look increasingly unrealistic.

A Legacy from the New Order System

By taking a few steps back and considering the previous impact of the New Order on Indonesia, we get some clues as to how and why political elites were able to manage the transition on their terms. For instance, NU and Muhammadiyah are massive socioreligious associations capable of huge mobilization, but the New Order hamstrung any political aspirations they may have had. There was also a conspicuous lack of conventional broad-based associations like trade unions.

It was in large part Suharto's ascendancy to power in 1965 that brought with it a brutal purge of leftists. Suharto went on to prohibit virtually all membership-based organizations autonomous of the government in a systematic attempt to fragment and isolate them from the general populace. His restructuring of the electoral system in 1971 also meant he could co-opt and control political activity within the structure of New Order corporatism. The notable exceptions were, of course, NU and Muhammadiyah but only on the condition that they did not agitate for political change.

This sweeping away of dissent effectively paralyzed the capacity for self-organization among urban middle-class and working-class groups (Uhlin 1997; Robison and Hadiz 2004). In short, there were extremely limited avenues of state-level political representation for marginal and disenfranchised sections of the population. New Order intransigence and suppression meant that anyone brave enough to oppose the New Order did so indirectly by promoting human rights, alternative NGO development, or single issues such as environmental problems and poverty. The systematic decontestation of societal identity vis-à-vis the state may go some way to explain why the student protests, despite being a powerful voice for change, failed in their efforts to organize an effective electoral challenge against political elites in 1999.

TRANSITION, PARTIES, AND ELECTIONS

To elaborate, by 1996, the state-sanctioned PDI was splitting apart. The choice approved by the New Order, Suryadi, had just gained the leadership ahead of the more popular Megawati Sukarnoputri at the party's Medan convention. This caused such consternation among the Sukarnoputri rank-and-file as to spark riots when police raided their Jakarta offices in July 1996. In the ensuing chaos, the death of several dozens of her supporters persuaded Megawati to break with elite consensus and take the political fight to Suharto as the figurehead of the newly formed PDI-P.

By 1997, momentum for political change had spread countrywide in the wake of the devastating Asian Financial Crisis (AFC). Suharto announced the annual budget in January 1998, much of which ran counter to the IMF guidelines for aid agreed in October 1997. The IMF-approved loan package had required Indonesia to reform its economy, end many state subsidies, and reduce cronyism. Instead, Suharto announced heavy subsidies for pet projects. This prompted IMF head Michael Camdessus to fly into Jakarta to get Suharto to sign a fresh letter of intent and fulfil IMF obligations. The nature of this meeting and subsequent media publicity fatally undermined Suharto's political credibility despite his reelection to a seventh presidential term. With the full effects of the AFC taking hold, events spiralled out of control. Rising food prices led to rioting in East and West Java, Sulawesi, Sumbawa, and Lombok. Suharto seemed incapable of assuaging public anger, and the increasing protests began to polarize the armed forces. An intramilitary power struggle developed between General Wiranto and General Prabowo Subianto (Suharto's son-in-law). Prabowo wanted a military-imposed solution to the demonstrations, while Wiranto urged more moderation. This threatened to split the army, with Wiranto's troops provisionally protecting the students from attacks by *Kopassus* and *Kostrad* under Prabowo. The day after Suharto stepped aside on May 21, 1998, Prabowo lost his command as head of *Kostrad* but Wiranto remained chief of the armed forces.

These short-lived and turbulent events removed Suharto, but they did not deliver wholesale change.

Ironically, however, the questionable legitimacy of B. J. Habibie's accession to power did help facilitate democratic concessions. The lifting of press restrictions, release of political prisoners, and the formation of new political parties all bore witness to a climate of reform. Yet, as the democratization literature points out, compromises struck during such periods can often end up serving the interests of established elites (Karl 1990: 1–23).

For instance, in Indonesia the military's nationalist *merah putih* (red and white) faction remained a dominant force. In particular, an influential group called the Pendawa Lima including the likes of now president Susilo Bambang Yudhoyono (SBY), Major-General Hendropriyono, General Wiranto, Major-General Agum Gumelar, and Major-General Farid Zainuddin retained close links to major political and economic players. Hendropriyono, for instance, had especially close ties to Suharto's son Bambang Trihatmojo and his Vice President Try Sutrisno. Similarly, Wiranto and Gumelar were close to Defence Minister Edi Sudrajat. Mochtar Pabottingi (*Tempo*, January 6, 2002) noted that Habibie's government was a change of government as usual but not a change of regime. Yet, the Habibie

"Interregnum" did seek compromise between established elites and an elite opposition. With the military looming large, established political elites were aware they would have to broker reform with them first and frantically set about negotiating alliances with the old regime in order to secure an advantage in the run up to the 1999 elections.

By May 1999, when demonstrations began to lose support from the moderate opposition, hope of a student-led *reformasi* began to wane. Significantly, however, political space had opened in the confusion surrounding Suharto's downfall. The leaders of the moderate opposition were able to take advantage of the pressure the student protests had put on a disoriented regime. This allowed them to pursue a negotiated but more limited programme of reform. Although the students may have viewed the willingness of the Ciganjur Four to do business with elements of the old regime as a breach of trust, they really had little choice.

At the same time, large numbers of radical democrats and student leaders failed to benefit in representative terms from the momentum of popular protests (Lane 1999: 239–251). For instance, NGOs like the Legal Aid Institute (LBH), Democracy Forum, or the Institute for the Defence of Human Rights lacked common platforms or sufficient coordination to mount a credible electoral challenge. Similarly, labor activists like Dita Sari, released from prison by Habibie, and her Indonesian Centre for Labour Struggle (PPBI—Pusat Perjuangan Buruh Indonesia) were given little or no time to organize in an electoral sense. With the majority of activists remaining outside the newly negotiated party political structure, the result was the effective exclusion of radical democratic agendas from the 1999 elections. This did not, however, stop them from continuing to campaign on issues like *korupsi, kolusi, nepotisme* (KKN—corruption, cronyism, and nepotism).

By contrast, in the run-up to election time, Megawati Sukarnoputri and Abdurrahman Wahid emerged as serious candidates for the highest office. Indonesians perceived both of them as respected figures whom they could trust. This allowed Sukarnoputri and Wahid to adopt explicitly populist approaches. Similarly, Amien Rais stood down from Muhammadiyah to take up the leadership of the National Mandate Party (PAN—Partai Amanat Nasional) in an attempt to appeal to Muslim middle-class constituencies. In the immediate postelection period, Habibie's interregnum lasted a mere seventeen months before the newly elected MPR rejected his presidential accountability speech by 355 votes to 322. By October 1999, Wahid had played a significant role in brokering talks with incumbent elites to forge a future without Habibie. Yet, the new deal struck between the old guard and the moderate opposition was one of restricted access and limited accountability.

To elaborate, existing electoral arrangements had given the military thirty-eight preallocated seats in parliament in 1999, four more than the popularly elected PAN. And despite Abdurrahman Wahid's Partai Kebangkitan Bangsa (PKB—National Awakening Party) having a mass base, it received only 8 percent of the seats in the MPR. In fact, 34 percent of the delegates, who eventually elected Abdurrahman Wahid president in October 1999, were not themselves directly elected but appointed by the military and political elite in Jakarta.

In fact, the controversial Wahid presidency (1999–2001) indicated a process still very much in transition, with elements in military and business elites maneuvering against him. This meant that his presidency was always on rocky ground. Wahid's impeachment after twenty-one months in office seemed somewhat of a fait accompli. On the other hand, although a state of normality had barely settled over the political system when this happened, Wahid, and subsequently, Megawati were still able to introduce significant constitutional and decentralization reforms. This restructuring meant that traditional elites had to operate within a democratic framework. In fact, rather than the impeachment signaling a return to authoritarian ways, it became the first big test of Indonesia's new democratic credentials. Parliament followed constitutional protocol and Vice President Megawati Sukarnoputri replaced Wahid to complete the remainder of the five-year presidential term.

The introduction of list-proportional representation also virtually assured that no party could secure a clear majority in parliament. This gave minority parties the chance to translate their share of votes into representation via coalition governments. For example, the Megawati government (2001–2004) comprised representation from nearly all the major parties in the assembly. As a further concession to moderate Muslim sensibilities, she appointed Hamzah Haz from the PPP as her vice president. A raft of constitutional amendments followed in 2002 that agreed further alterations to the composition of parliament and governmental process. Significantly, these amendments formalized powers for the eventual removal of the military's guaranteed political representation in parliament and a mandate for a directly elected president.

Despite reforms, voters had to choose representatives from party lists and, therefore, tended to opt for a party rather than a specific candidate. Unfortunately, the politicians were often more concerned about their position on the appropriate party list rather than the concerns of their constituency. Having said this, 2004 did herald a directly elected president who can only serve one renewable five-year term. The president-elect now has to win over 50 percent of the total vote with a minimum of 20 percent in at least half the provinces. This is something that forces candidates to secure widespread popular support across the archipelago. The thinking behind this is that it encourages moderate candidates who can appeal to different interests and form alliances across party lines.

Parliament also has greater powers to veto legislation and limit presidential power. This obliges the president to maintain broad support in the legislature. The 2004 election also inaugurated the new Regional Representatives Council (DPD—Dewan Perwakilan Daerah). Although with extremely limited powers, it does constitute, in a narrow sense, a second chamber of elected representatives. Interestingly, the DPD's majoritarian, single nontransferable vote system differs from the list proportionality of the Dewan Perwakilan Raykat (DPR—House of Representative). Each province makes up an electoral district with candidates standing individually rather than as members of a political party. The problem with this is that although it increases contestation, it has the potential to create a new layer of corruption with new provincial political elites seeking to maintain their patronage links with Jakarta.

Evidently, institutionalization within a more representative party system is a "two steps forward one step back" kind of process. Taking a quick look at the fringes of national politics, we can see a number of minor opposition parties that represent labor interests, but they have struggled to consolidate much of a political base. Dr. Sri Bintang Pamungkas' Partai Uni Demokrasi Indonesia (PUDI—Democratic Unity Party–Indonesia) and labor activists, Dr. Mochtar Pakpahan's Partai Buruh Nasional (PBN—National Labour Party) and Wilhelmus Bhoka's Partai Pekerja Indonesia (PPI—The Indonesian Workers' Party), have some influence in Jakarta, especially with the industrial working class and intellectuals, but little broad appeal.

As suggested earlier, developing political constituencies around a common platform is difficult due to a lack of organized interest-based movements. For instance, if one looks at the experience of Megawati Sukarnoputri's PDI-P, the problem is all too clear. Given her lineage, Megawati played a key role in the transition. She had wide appeal allowing her to garner support from rural, urban middle class, and working-class constituencies. Yet, her PDI-P party failed to engage and maintain this mass support after the elections of 1999. It was organizationally weak and lacked an effective party structure capable of redefining the political landscape. Golkar's institutional machinery had remained largely intact despite Suharto's downfall. This gave them control of foreign-funded credits for cooperatives and social safety-net programmes. This meant that PDI-P could do little to challenge the reach of Golkar's patronage and hegemony. The seeming naivety and stagnation of the Megawati presidency compounded the failure to consolidate its popular appeal. As a result, there was significant erosion of the PDI-P vote in 2004. Ironically, PDI-P's waning popularity benefited the party that did so much to maintain Suharto in power. Despite its association with the discredited regime of Suharto, Golkar did not suffer the loss of public support that PDI-P experienced.

Golkar may no longer be the corporatist enforcer of old will, but it still wields considerable power. Its distinctive organizational structure and massive patronage networks facilitated a reemergence in the new political system. In 2004, Golkar achieved 21.6 percent of the vote, compared to 22.5 percent in 1999, but PDI-P's share dropped from 33.7 percent to 18.5 percent. This meant that Golkar gained 128 of the 550 seats in the DPR (up from 120 in 1999) compared to PDI-P's 109 seats (down from 153 in 1999). Its reinvention as a regionalist political party also means that it has retained a strong presence in local legislatures.

Conclusion

Constitutional reforms aside, the political euphoria that accompanied a crumbling authoritarian regime raised expectations very high in Indonesia. The compromises necessary to ensure relative stability and a peaceful transition were always going to disappoint in some respects. As we can see, legacies of the past are resilient and can produce modified forms of continuation. Despite a "new" social contract, patronage and old loyalties do persist. In many cases, community interests remain marginalized and relatively subordinated to the interests of local patrons of national parties. These situations are no more keenly felt than in provinces like Kalimantan and Papua Barat (West Papua). The most troubling prognosis could be something similar to the Philippines, where bossism and money politics hold sway. On the other hand, Golkar, as a former hegemonic presence, may display formidable institutional strengths, but, as mentioned in Chapter 5, its past has also imbued it with some distinctive and unmistakable weaknesses. What Partai Demokrat's (PD—Democratic Party) election victory in 2009 indicates is that Golkar's earlier electoral success in the post-Suharto era was more a product of uneven institutionalization than unequivocal institutional strength on its part.

On the other hand, one of the encouraging effects of democratization in Indonesia is the acknowledgement of the regions with the party system developing to include elections to the new regional representatives council. There is now a greater degree of local representation than in the past. In this context, the next chapter considers the implications of decentralization within Indonesia's constitutional framework.

PART IV

THE EFFECT OF DECENTRALIZATION

CHAPTER 7

DEMOCRATIZATION AND
DECENTRALIZATION

Transitions from authoritarian rule bring with them a mixture of anticipation and concern. Indonesia is certainly no exception. Yet, thankfully, in the intervening years, the archipelago has transformed itself into the world's third-largest democracy. Having said this, some influential commentators do voice very legitimate concerns about the level of oligarchic reorganization within the new framework of democratic institutions (Hadiz 2003: 591–611; Robison and Hadiz 2004). They view the ability of Suharto-era predatory interests to secure new political allies as effectively emasculating institutional and policy reform (Hadiz 2004: 55–71). In short, this is a hijacking of the consolidation process (Hadiz and Robison 2005: 220–241).

It is undoubtedly an important task to highlight these trends, but we need to tread carefully when drawing conclusions on the kind of democracy establishing itself. In fact, to conclude that Indonesian democratization is more akin to a reinstatement of powerful constellations of state and politico-business oligarchs through new institutions relies too heavily on a particular understanding of transition dynamics. An understanding that assumes that social change and the institutions established in its wake are structurally conditioned and causally contingent on a struggle between salient socioeconomic forces.

It is over a decade since Indonesia's initial transition, and it now seems appropriate to further consider institutional reorganization in the country. This chapter questions a primarily structural approach to understanding transition dynamics. It highlights the importance of focusing on unravelling the interplay between political action and institutions to appreciate the complexity of the unfolding process. This is because human actors who shape change in particular settings must turn structural factors into political resources of enactment (Kim, Liddle, and Said 2006: 247–268). An important question to ask then is whether the interplay actually begins to undermine oligarchic dominance democratically or reinscribes it. This is a tricky question to answer for sure, especially as Indonesia's transformation, along with other democratizations, is anything but straightforward. In fact, it is probably safer to say there are no simple categorizations, but rather matters of time and degree. And in Indonesia's case, the tactical decision to alter the highly centralized state structures of the Suharto era is just one step forward in an uneven process (Alm, Aten, and Bahl 2001: 83–102). Yet, the introduction of this crucial, albeit limited, variable to the political system has lessened the effectiveness of oligarchic reorganization.

HISTORICAL LEGACIES AND LEGITIMACY

Before going any further, I need to give a bit of background on the significance of Indonesia's decision to decentralize. To begin with, the archipelago is amazingly diverse, both geographically and ethnodemographically. Despite this, historically, political elites have resisted representational challenges to their authority. For them, either you have power or you do not. In fact, powerful constituencies, especially the military, are deeply suspicious of politico-territorial fragmentation (Ferrazzi 2000: 63–85). Their strong commitment to a unified political identity is, in the main, born out of the anticolonial struggle for independence (Bertrand 2004). This is something reflected in the institutional centralization of the nation-state and the postindependence rule of both Sukarno and Suharto. But it was Suharto, in particular, who depoliticized societal identity vis-à-vis a form of centralized state corporatism. He achieved this through a combination of co-optation and repression (Ford 2000: 59–88). In this context, the introduction of the decentralization initiative is a considerable achievement for and alteration to Indonesian politics.

To elaborate, the bulk of Suharto's legitimacy rested on the promise of stability and economic growth rather than on any sort of representative plurality. As mentioned in earlier chapters, to shore this up and remove threats to his regime, he also set about the social construction of a "floating mass" populace (*massa mengambang*). This involved the systemic disorganization of civil society by banning political activity at the village level and either suppressing or co-opting membership-based organizations autonomous of the government—when one compares the relevance of forms of collective organization to the growth of democracy in other developing countries, the decision to decentralize Indonesia's political system appears even more significant.

At the same time, Suharto went on to operationalize his dominance over the state administration through a conglomeration of functional groups. Sitting at the apex of this political structure, he went on to extend state patronage across the archipelago through Golkar and a vast network of state officials and business interests (MacIntyre 1991). Access to state revenues came via these patronage networks, all of which remained firmly attached to a highly centralized corporatist style of rule. In fact, the 1970s and early 1980s boom in resource exports shielded, for a time at least, the viability of this form of rule from international market realities. As long as public revenues from the likes of Pertamina, the state-owned oil and gas monopoly, kept flowing, they underwrote the economic success story. In the meantime, Suharto, an archetypal "crony capitalist," used state companies as cash cows for his family members and close associates.

Nevertheless, even as oil monies poured in, foreign investment fell in the face of restrictively high subsidies given to state-owned companies (Hill 1999). As the state control mechanisms began to creak under the pressure of globalization, rumblings of elite dissension emerged. Indonesia's violent convulsion in the wake of the 1997 Asian Financial Crisis (AFC) brutally exposed the friability of Suharto's style of patrimonial corporatism. It effectively short-circuited the patronage networks, and, as the crisis of regime legitimacy worsened, Suharto's corporatist grip looked increasingly unsustainable.

Difficult Steps and Strategic Interactions

Given this context, the time for some strategic decisions had arrived. Suharto's successor, B. J. Habibie, would go on to play a significant "soft-liner" role during the transition from authoritarian rule and, in some respects, facilitated further democratic opening. As David Bourchier

(2000: 15) notes, Habibie "presided over a remarkable and almost Gorbachevesque period of political reform" between May 1998 and November 1999. The impetus was more a mixture of pragmatism and fear of grassroot insurrection, but it did make democratic compromise possible. Habibie certainly lacked outright legitimacy as the new president; this meant he had little strategic alternative other than compromise. His attempts to reestablish legitimate credentials paved the way for moderate opposition elites to step onto the political playing field. They included Nahdlatul Ulama's (NU) Abdurrahman Wahid, Sukarno's daughter Megawati Sukarnoputri, Muhammadiyah's Amien Rais, and the Sultan of Yogyakarta, Hamengkubuwono X.

As the democratization literature indicates, it is in situations like these that a critical juncture of compromise between elite political figures can develop, especially when faced with popular pressure from below (Karl and Schmitter 1991: 274). This in turn creates political space out of which unexpected policy reform and unintended outcomes emerge. In similar contexts, democratization and some form of elite power-sharing is a practical strategy for managing societal tensions. Ideally, such power-sharing and territorial decentralization allows the institutional means for conflict within a society to be managed nonviolently (Byman 2002: 126). In the Indonesian case, Habibie's decision to redefine territorial boundaries and devolve government authority is one such example. This unprecedented attempt to manage growing societal pressure created an unanticipated adjustment to structural asymmetries.

INDEPENDENCE FOR EAST TIMOR

One of the root causes of unrest in Indonesia is that marginalized groups lack access to resources and legitimate representation (Colombijn and Lindblad 2002). For example, between 1997 and 1999, with the full effects of the AFC ripping a swathe across the archipelago, ethnoreligious violence erupted in Kalimantan, Sulawesi, and the Mulukus and tensions flared in the separatist hotspots of East Timor, Aceh, and Papua Barat (West Papua) (Malley 2002: 170–189). Indeed, separatist demands reached such an extent in East Timor that in an unprecedented volte-face the Habibie government decided to hold an independence referendum in 1999.

Despite a referendum marred by violence and intimidation, some 78 percent of the East Timorese population voted for independence. This historic vote created the new Republika Demokratika Timor Lorosa'e (Democratic Republic of Timor-Leste) and led to a major redefinition of Indonesia's territorial boundaries. Having said this, gauging whether it is enough to heal the scars of the past is more difficult. In fact, the process of reconciliatory justice will be a long one if a recent report sent to the United Nations by the East Timorese Commission for Reception, Truth and Reconciliation is anything to go by. It estimates that 183,000 East Timorese died during Indonesia's 25 years of occupation. To date, the Indonesia military has largely avoided recriminations, with only a small number of military officers convicted at the 2002 Ad-Hoc Court for Human Rights Violations in East Timor (Linton 2004: 303–361). Three of the high-ranking officers responsible for issuing orders in East Timor, General Wiranto (defence minister at the time), Major-General Zacky Anwar Makarim, and Lieutenant-General Kiki Syahnakri avoided trial. The United Nations' Human Rights Tribunal (SCU— Serious Crimes Unit) did eventually issue warrants against General Wiranto and six other senior army officers in 2004. There is, however, little chance of their enforcement.

For Timor-Leste the long, slow process of nation building has really just begun.

SPECIAL AUTONOMY IN ACEH

Significantly, another unexpected outcome of the Indonesian transition is the change that also came to places like Aceh. It is another Indonesian province with a strong sense of identity and proud history of resistance against Dutch colonialism. Unfortunately, postindependence, the nationalist project failed to accommodate its sense of autonomy and subordinated the province to the interests of the unitary republic (Bertrand 2004: 161–163). Both Sukarno and Suharto siphoned off rich oil and gas revenues to serve interests in Java and Sumatra. This exploitation of resources left not only a sense of deep resentment and disenfranchisement but extensive environmental degradation (Tiwon 2000: 97–104). From 1976, the Free Aceh Movement (GAM—Gerakan Aceh Merdeka) mounted an armed struggle for independence that met with a campaign of violent repression by the Indonesian military (Budiardjo 2001: 1–8).

Since August 2001, however, the introduction of special autonomy legislation (Law No. 18) has given both provinces a greater share of resource revenues and increased say over their own affairs. In the case of Aceh, this included 80 percent of the forest and oil revenues and 70 percent of mine revenues. This scale of revenue redistribution is not without difficulties. Aceh itself comprises 17 regencies, four city municipalities, 147 subdistricts, and 5,529 villages. They all vie for key political positions and access to income revenue. Northern Aceh is keen for more revenue, and central and southern Aceh continue to feel that the provincial government in Banda Aceh ignores their interests.

Endemic corruption means the risk of revenue distribution abuse is also high. Aceh does now have a Wali Nanggroe (symbolic head of state). Although this position carries no political powers, it helps embody the distinct history and traditions of the province. There is also a form of "legal pluralism" with the partial implementation and limited jurisdiction of Shari'a under Law 18/2001 and Presidential Decree 11/2003. *Mahkamah Syar' iyah* (Shari'a Courts) now deal with Muslim civil and criminal cases National courts, however, retain jurisdiction over non-Muslims, the security forces, and civil servants.

In tandem with these developments, and of much wider significance, was the possibility of a negotiated settlement to the long conflict in Aceh. In fact, Indonesia's own democratic transition seemed to introduce a new political dialectic with Jakarta embarking on a strategy of negotiation and repression. In 2000, President Wahid demonstrated a willingness to hold talks with rebel leaders but the military continued to suppress (Ariffadhillah 2001: 317–331). Wahid supported the idea of talks with GAM under the mediation of the Henri Dunant Centre (HDC). The involvement of a third party was a symbolically significant step because it showed a commitment to negotiate. Unfortunately, despite the signing by both parties of a Joint Understanding for a one-month "humanitarian pause" in May 2000, the conflict covertly continued. Negotiations eventually stalled due to the fragility of Wahid's authority.

In the wake of Wahid's impeachment in July 2001, the military immediately arrested six GAM delegates involved in the peace talks and the death toll increased. Yet, several members of the newly installed Megawati cabinet were instrumental in recommending direct negotiations with GAM, namely, Foreign Minister Hasan Wirajuda and Susilo Bambang Yudhoyono, the then Minister for

Politics and Security. By August 2001, President Megawati Sukarnoputri had honored a commitment to introduce autonomy legislation for Aceh and Papua.

On December 9, 2002, the Indonesian government and GAM signed a Cessation of Hostilities Accord (COHA) in Geneva. But with GAM refusing to drop their independence demands and the failure of last minute talks in Tokyo, Megawati announced a six-month military emergency and martial law that was extended for another six months. Intentionally or otherwise, what the Indonesian elites had done, however, was establish a precedent for negotiation. The establishment of which can, in the long run, help facilitate trust, negotiation, and eventual cooperation (Draper 2002: 391–418; Singh 2000: 184–216).

Indeed, despite the attempts to impose a military solution in Aceh, the repressive strategies of old appeared increasingly unsustainable (Sukma 2003: 64–74). In the past, Suharto had simply suppressed regional demands, but new national and international realities seemed to demand a slightly different approach. Pragmatists in Jakarta even began to consider a political solution, especially after the tsunami of December 26, 2004, devastated Aceh, killing some 170,000, leaving 500,000 homeless and causing $4.5 billion worth of damage. And with mounting external pressure to resolve the conflict, representatives of GAM and Indonesia went back to the negotiating table under the auspices of the Crisis Management Initiative. Thanks largely to the efforts of former Finnish Prime Minister Martti Ahtissari, both sides eventually signed a memorandum of understanding on August 15, 2005, in Helsinki. This led to a ceasefire and amnesty for GAM members in return for decommissioning arms.

By late 2005, Indonesia had released some 1,500 GAM members from prison and withdrawn over 6,000 troops.

In contrast to other semiautonomous territories, Susilo Bambang Yudhoyono's (SBY) government also granted Aceh wider autonomy in 2006. This gives Aceh further access to resource revenues and allows it to field independent candidates for the election of provincial governor and district heads. After many false dawns and years of strife and rebellion, Aceh appears to be on a new road. Unfortunately, the story is not the same for the other special territory of Papua, designated by Law No. 21. Despite moves toward new territorial-administrative boundaries, the province's political representation is still firmly located within the unitary political framework. Only nationally registered parties can compete in elections, and it remains debatable whether this limited decompression strategy will reduce tensions there.

NATIONAL DECENTRALIZATION INITIATIVE

Putting East Timor and Aceh aside for a moment, the Indonesian transition was a period fraught with domestic tensions and dissatisfaction; tensions the institutional mechanisms of old seemed ill equipped to address. In an attempt to decompress these tensions, the Habibie government decided on a raft of decentralization (*desentralisasi*) reforms that introduced a political devolution of government authority with new fiscal and revenue-raising powers. For an ethnically heterogeneous Indonesia with a history of centralized authoritarian rule, this represented a way of devolving power from the centre to the regions and recognized the diversity of the nation without undermining its political identity. It was a process enacted through Laws No. 22/1999 (Regional Governance—Undang Undang Republik Indonesia Nomor 22 Tahun 1999 tentang "Pemerintahan Daerah") and No. 25/1999 (Fiscal

Arrangements—Undang Undang Republik Indonesia Nomor 25 Tahun 1999 tentang "Perimbangan Keuangan Antara Pemerintah Pusat dan Daera") and formally implemented on January 1, 2001, the intention being to promote *otonomi daerah* (regional autonomy) by making the province (*provinsi*), regency (*kabupaten*), and city (*kota*) political and fiscal players in the newly devolved structure.

This national decentralization initiative clearly represented an important step in Indonesia's democratization as a whole. However, it is usually best to measure such things by degrees. The overhaul of Suharto's intensely centralized power structure was never going to be a universal panacea. For instance, Golkar's administrative entrenchment weighed heavily in the newly devolved political structure (Smith 2001: 74–117). And the Indonesian Armed Forces (TNI—Tentara Nasional Indonesia) still exert a strong influence despite the constitutional removal of their dual function (*dwifungsi*) role. Their ability to maintain a quasi-political role remains a concern, and this is mainly due to their substantial business interests and continued links to major political players (McCulloch 2003: 94–124).

As a result, decentralization in Indonesia is subject to much legitimate criticism (Erb, Sulistiyanto, and Faucher 2005; Aspinall and Fealy 2003). In fact, the early optimism seemed more hope than expectation. From the outset, the 1999 legislation contained many inconsistencies, creating a recipe for confusion and poor implementation. This meant that its effectiveness varied widely across the archipelago. There was also the assumption that local governments would be better at dealing with local needs and problems. This proved to be a rather sanguine expectation, brought in to stark relief with the proliferation (*pemekaran*) of administrative districts.

Given the rapid expansion of new undertakings, existing institutional practice was, in some respects, inappropriately equipped to deal with it. Over a hundred subdivisions of regencies took place between 1999 and 2004, increasing the total number by roughly 50 percent. By 2005, 33 provinces and some 450 regencies and cities were in existence. This, along with a lack of guidelines from central government, led to significantly different takes on the new political and fiscal responsibilities. In some respects, *pemekaran* magnified rent-seeking behavior and revenue mismanagement (Fitrani, Hofman, and Kaiser 2005: 57–59). Many local administrations simply lacked the appropriate technical capacity and personnel. In fact, service delivery, instead of improving overnight, actually deteriorated in places like northern Sulawesi and southern Sumatra. Marginalization issues in Kalimantan and Sulawesi also did little to alleviate matters (Duncan 2007: 711–733). Another worrying trend is that local indigenous populations (*putra daerah*, native son) began demanding priority for regional government jobs, ahead of migratory newcomers (*pendatang*). On the other hand, the introduction of legislative amendments in October 2004 (Law No. 32/2004) has improved some of these shortcomings by placing renewed emphasis on addressing administrative disputes, budget mismanagement, local accountability, and closer monitoring by central government.

One thing is for sure: the politics of pragmatic change is anything but smooth. At the village level, formal political rights are one thing, exercising them is another. Corruption is still rife especially among local elites, with money appropriated from village projects, land certificates overcharged, public land privatized and public social safety nets misused. With little encouragement at the state level, villagers usually take it upon themselves to move against corrupt *kepala desa* (village head) and Golkar hegemony (Antlov 2003: 193–214; Tornquist 2000: 383–423). Villagers have set up reform committees (*komite reformasi*) to counter corrupt village heads, but they face many obstacles, most notably from established vested interests that largely remain in de facto control of local administrations.

Nevertheless, the political crafting of institutional change has done more than decant old wine into new bottles. The decentralized political system has helped widen intraelite competition, albeit by degrees. Despite ongoing rent-seeking behavior, new political configurations are more than a reassertion of oligarchy in a different guise. Representative contestation and accountability now extend to a broader range of both bureaucrats and local leaders. This means they are in competition politically for not only resources and taxation but also, ultimately, votes (Eckardt 2008: 1–17). Performance is beginning to matter, and this creates incentive, at least, to appear more inclusive and constituent friendly.

The upshot is an influence, however slight, on policy decisions and priorities. Multiple elites also mean that marriages of convenience and compromise take place between political parties with similar local interests but different national agendas. This involves, in certain instances, a putting aside of national differences to assert local governance against central interference. In other words, the increased contestation of regional politics brings with it a very gradual destabilization of the centralized nexus of political power.

In West Sumatra, for instance, a formidable Golkar party backed former Governor Zainal Bakar as he came from within the state bureaucracy. Yet, to pigeonhole Bakar as an exclusive reflection of "old" power would be somewhat misleading. His parliamentary allies represented a mixture of regional and national political interests. More significantly, the reputation for integrity of the new governor, Gamawan Fauzi, is a welcome fillip, especially given Bakar's implication in several corruption cases.

From a broader Huntingtonian (1991: 263) perspective, two consecutive free and fair elections and a transfer of power from incumbent opposition mean that Indonesia has passed a key litmus test of democratic consolidation. The 2004 elections, supported by an effective General Elections Commission (KPU—Komisi Pemilihan Umum), also heralded improved civilian rule over the military, allowed a meaningful and extensive number of permitted political parties, stabilized election rules, brought in amendments to the decentralization legislation, and imposed constitutional limitations on the power of the executive. Moreover, the inauguration of the new Regional Representatives Council (DPD—Dewan Perwakilan Daerah) is symbolically (and structurally) a significant step for improving representation. It creates, in effect, a bicameral second chamber of parliament. This acts as a sort of upper house, albeit with extremely limited powers and no veto over the budget.

Altering the composition of parliament may eventually lessen regional distrust of central government. For instance, since 2004, the restructured People's Consultative Assembly (MPR—Majelis Permusyawaratan Rakyat) consists entirely of popularly elected members sitting in the People's Representative Council (DPR—Dewan Perwakilan Rakyat) and the new DPD. In theory, there is the potential to give Indonesia's diverse communities a greater representational presence in Jakarta.

Likewise, since 2005, *pilkada* (local elections) for hundreds of *gubernur* (governors), *bupati* (regents/district heads), and *walikota* (city mayors) have certainly altered the political landscape, with about 40 percent of incumbents replaced. Whether there has been a dramatic change in the new incumbents' representational priorities is, however, harder to gauge. Yet, greater competition for office, logistically at least, represents a gradual dilution of the system of top-down executive appointments and manipulated assembly votes. This is not to say things are all plain sailing. In terms of institutionalization, the party system is still captive to personality politics and most parties are widely seen as corrupt and self-interested (Johnson Tan 2006: 88–114).

On the other hand, the president and vice president now have to stand as a team. This is supposed to encourage moderate candidates who have the capacity to form alliances across party lines (Liddle and Mujani 2006: 132–139). Although SBY is ex-military, he is politically acute and displays a commitment to the new democratic framework (McBride 2004). In fact, this explains a lot about his choice of Golkar's Jusuf Kalla as vice president in 2004. And while SBY is big on rhetoric, he has at least sought to stabilize the economy and combat corruption (Hill and Shiraishi 2007: 123–141).

In a Przeworskian sense, SBY readily submits his interests and values to the uncertain interplay of democratic institutions. He also shows little fear in reshuffling his cabinet and disrupting the cozy political cartel of previous administrations. Recent infusions of high-level civilian technocratic expertise reinforce this point. For instance, in 2005, he replaced Coordinating Minister for the Economy Aburizal Bakrie (head of the Bakrie Brothers conglomerate, a major economic vehicle of the Suharto era) with Dr. Boediono. The DPR also approved Boediono's nomination as the new governor of Bank Indonesia (BI) in April 2008, and he is presently SBY's vice presidential running mate for the upcoming presidential election. Likewise, prominent economist Dr. Sri Mulyani Indrawati came in as the new finance minister, with SBY backing her anti-corruption drive. Indrawati has already sacked her director-general of taxation in 2006 and lately overhauled the customs staff at Tanjung Priok port (MacDonald 2007).

The inroads against Indonesia's endemic nexus of corruption and graft are, however, more meager. One merely has to consider the scandals surrounding the Indonesian Bank Restructuring Agency (IBRA), the National Logistics Agency (Bulog—*Badan Urusan Logistik Nasional*), or the Bank Indonesia Liquidity Assistance (BLBI) to appreciate the scale of the problem. Attempts to rein in the conglomerates of the Suharto era remain fraught and uneven. The findings of the Supreme Audit Agency (BPK—Badan Pemeriksa Keuangan) and investigations by the Corruption Eradication Commission (KPK—Komisi Pemberantasan Korupsi) reflect this fact (Mulia 2008). For instance, the Attorney General's Office decided to drop charges against two major BLBI debtors, Sjamsul Nursalim and Anthony Salim due to a lack of evidence. But the KPK recently detained prosecutor Urip Tri Gunawan, business executive Artalita Suryani, lawmaker Hamka Yamdu, and Jambi Deputy Governor Anthony Zeidra Abidin in connection to the BLBI case.

CONCLUSION

Evidently, countries do not emerge from authoritarianism to multiparty democracy overnight. Indeed, the way political actors alter and reconstitute disarticulated political space can both enable and constrain the kind of democracy establishing itself. At the same time, the activity of politics does bring with it a stabilizing combination of pragmatism and compromise. In the Indonesian case, despite the complicated challenges, the reform crafted by political elites, over time, has made a renegotiation of improved representation possible. In fact, elite behavior does display modification to widening contestation, and no matter how constrained the potential, this has improved the system of governance. On balance, then, we can say the institutional reform of the post-Suharto political system is, albeit modestly, destabilizing oligarchic proclivities rather than simply facilitating their retrenchment. What this highlights is the complex roles both political action and institutions play in postauthoritarian settings, a process that is rarely, if ever, ideal.

CHAPTER 8

CONCLUSION

The literature suggests that the outcome of a "pact" transition depends, in part, on the nature of the foundational bargain (Karl 1990: 15). And while this mode of transition may afford a degree of stability, the trade-off is a series of compromises that generally weigh in favour of established elites (Karl and Schmitter 1991: 274). As the Indonesian case demonstrates, mass protests did provide a catalyst for change, but despite this, political elites still managed to maintain a level of control over the transition. In other words, major reform took place, but political elites simultaneously reinvented their roles according to rules that emerged in contingent circumstances of change.

This book has sought to unravel how and why this happened. It established that in Indonesia, multiple conditioning factors including authoritarian legacies, *politik aliran*, Islamic identity politics, new middle-class allegiances, and decentralization reform both enabled and constrained the journey from authoritarianism. Although far from an ideal situation, this is not necessarily a negative outcome.

After all, from a Przeworskian perspective, successful democratization is really about relevant political forces finding how best to continue to submit their interests and values to the uncertain interplay of democratic institutions. Despite all its faults, what Indonesia's ambiguous blend of continuity, change, and uncertainty indicates is a process well on its way. There may be policy ineffectiveness, executive mismanagement, judicial problems, institutional frictions, endemic corruption, and reserved domains but, as this book has shown, the new political system is not only qualitatively different from the Suharto era but also accepted.

To checklist Dahl's criteria, Indonesia's first two elections in 1999 and 2004 were the freest in more than forty years with huge amounts of political activity and media coverage. The success of the 2009 legislative elections also attests to real consolidation. There has been a significant redefinition of state boundaries with Indonesia relinquishing annexation of East Timor in October 1999 in accordance with the UN-organised referendum on August 30, 1999. On the domestic front, the media remain open and vigorous. Civil society activity continues to flourish with a vast array of NGOs and pressure groups. Factor in major constitutional and decentralization reform and there is now far greater representation and accountability than under Suharto. In fact, the now directly elected president can only serve one renewable five-year term. Constitutional limitations on the power of the executive and more power for parliament to amend, or veto legislation also encourages the president to maintain broad support in the legislature.

Moreover, although the military and business elites flexed their muscles in the early years of the transition, especially during Wahid's controversial presidency (1999–2001), they did accept new reforms. For instance, by 2004, the restructured MPR consisted entirely of popularly elected members and approval from the DPR was necessary for the appointment and dismissal of the commander of the military and chief of police. This is not to say that the military simply and quietly retreated to the barracks, but it does indicate a willingness to operate within new rules. To a large extent, they have started to promote their political agendas according to civilian rule. Susilo Bambang Yudhoyono's (SBY) government even introduced further measures to reduce military involvement in big business in 2005.

Similarly, decentralization is a complex and challenging process, but competition for office has increased. The fight against endemic *korupsi, kolusi,* and *nepotisme* (corruption, cronyism, and nepotism) may be as fraught as ever, but there are certain inroads. On September 4, 2002, for example, a court convicted Akbar Tandjung, the ex-head of Golkar, of using 40 billion rupiah ($8m) of National Logistics Agency (Bulog—*Badan Urusan Logistik Nasional*) nonbudgetary funds earmarked for poverty relief to finance Golkar's 1999 election campaign. Granted the Supreme Court eventually exonerated him on February 12, 2004, but it did irreparable damage to his electoral credibility. More importantly, greater transparency in accounting standards and an independent commission to prosecute corruption emerged in the wake of the farrago.

One of the biggest surprises on the new political landscape has been the rise of SBY and his Partai Demokrat (PD—Democratic Party). PD's arrival onto the political stage in 2004 under the charismatic leadership of SBY hinted at a growing influence from Indonesia's middle classes. This influence certainly played out in 2009 with an unprecedented legislative election victory for PD. Voters turned away in their droves from established political parties and found a credible alternative in PD.

The scale of the victory could indicate a new phase in Indonesia's democratic consolidation. This may force established elites to change their usual proclivities if they wish to remain politically competitive. Of course, a real overriding danger, however, is that corruption continues unabated in politics and state institutions. In fact, Indonesians are under no illusions that the journey is over.

It does seem that a major lesson from the Indonesian experience is that ambiguity is to democratization what push is to shove. Yet, merely to state this raises difficult questions of interpretation. For a start, democratization does not derive exclusively from a free play of unconstrained political action. There are complex local terrains with multiple conditioning factors to consider, all of which affect decisions and strategies of change in different ways. This leaves us asking how to map what is essentially a complex interplay between context and agency.

I hope what this book has demonstrated is the need to carefully navigate both the implicit voluntarism of an actor-agency school of thought and the determinism of structural analysis. This involves linking the wider democratization literature to a specific context in a way that reflects the centrality of debates about structure and agency. What the book attempted to do was give a fine-grained reading of Indonesia's grammar of political action and the material and ideational factors in play during its renegotiated post-authoritarian settlement.

This seems an important step to take, because it redirects our attention toward rigorous epistemic plurality and the stimulation of collegial dialogue. If we learn from different experiences and perspectives, we can improve our chances of coming to grips with the ambiguous relationship between agency and narratives of history, culture, and identity in the study of democratization. It may even shorten the distance between theory and reality.

References

Books, Book Chapters, and Journal Articles

Alavi, H., P. Burns, G. Knight, P. Mayer, and D. McEachern. 1982. *Capitalism and colonial production*. London: Croom Helm.

Alm, J., R. Aten, and R. Bahl. 2001. Can Indonesia decentralize successfully? Plans, problems and prospects. *Bulletin of Indonesian Economic Studies* 37(1): 83–102.

Anderson, B. 1972. The idea of power in Javanese culture. *Culture and Politics in Indonesia*. C. Holt, ed. Ithaca, NY: Cornell University Press.

———. 1990. *Language and power: Exploring political cultures in Indonesia*. Ithaca, NY: Cornell University Press.

———. 1991. *Imagined communities: Reflections on the origin and spread of nationalism*. London and New York: Verso.

———. 2001. *Violence and the state in Suharto's Indonesia*. Ithaca, NY: Southeast Asia Program Publications, Southeast Asia Program, Cornell University.

Antlov, H. 1995. *Exemplary centre, administrative periphery: Rural leadership and the New Order in Java*. Richmond, UK: Curzon Press.

———. 2000. Demokrasi Pancasila and the future of ideology in Indonesia. *The cultural construction of politics in Asia*. H. Antlov and T. W. Ngo, eds., 203–222. New York: St Martin's Press.

———. 2003b. Village government and rural development in Indonesia: The new democratic framework. *Bulletin of Indonesian Economic Studies* 39(2): 193–214.

Antlov, H., and S. Cederroth. 2004. *Elections in Indonesia: The New Order and beyond*. London: RoutledgeCurzon.

Arief, S., and A. Sasono. 1973. *Indonesia: Dependency and underdevelopment*. Kuala Lumpur: META.

Ariffadhillah. 2001. The recent situation in Aceh. *Violence in Indonesia*. Wessel, I., and G. Wimhofer, eds., 317–331. Hamburg: Abera Publishing House.

Aspinall, E., and G. Fealy, eds. 2003. *Local power and politics in Indonesia: Decentralisation and democratisation*. Singapore: Institute of Southeast Asian Studies.

Azra, A. 2000. The Islamic factor in post-Soeharto Indonesia. *Indonesia in transition: Social aspects of reformasi and crisis.* C. Manning and P. van Diermen, eds., 309–318. Singapore: Institute of Southeast Asian Studies.

———. 2001. Islam, politics and regime change in Wahid's Indonesia. *Tiger's Roar: Asia's recovery and its impact.* J. Weiss, ed., 312–317. London: ME Sharpe.

———. 2002. Islam and politics in the new Indonesia. *Islam and Asia: Changing political realities.* J. Isaacson and C. Rubenstein, eds., 1–90. New Brunswick, NJ: Transaction Publishers.

Barton, G., and G. Fealy. 1996. *Nadhlatul Ulama, traditional Islam and modernity in Indonesia.* Melbourne: Monash Asia Institute.

Basri, M. 1999. Indonesia: The political economy of policy reform. Reformasi: *Crisis and change in Indonesia.* A. Budiman, B. Hatley, and D. Kingsbury, eds., 27–37. Melbourne: Monash Asia Institute.

Bermeo, N. 1990. Rethinking regime change. *Comparative Politics* 22: 359–377.

———. 1997. Myths of moderation: Confrontation and conflict during democratic transitions. *Comparative Politics* 29(3): 305–322.

Bertrand, J. 2004. *Nationalism and ethnic conflict in Indonesia.* Cambridge: Cambridge University Press.

Bjork, C. 2003. Local responses to decentralization policy in Indonesia. *Comparative Education Review* 47(2): 184–216.

Boas, F. [1940] 1988. *Race, language, and culture.* Chicago: University of Chicago Press.

Bourchier, D. 2000. Habibie's interregnum: *Reformasi,* elections, regionlism and the struggle for power. *Indonesia in transition: Social aspects of* Reformasi *and crisis.* C. Manning and P. van Diermen, eds., 15–38. Singapore: Institute of Southeast Asian Studies.

Bunce, V. 2000. Comparative democratisation: Big and bounded generalisations. *Comparative Political Studies* 33(6–7): 703–734.

Byman, D. 2002. *Keeping the peace: Lasting solutions to ethnic conflicts.* Baltimore: John Hopkins University Press.

Cardoso, F. H. and E. Faletto. 1979. *Dependency and development in Latin America.* Trans. M. Mattingly Urquidi. Berkeley: University of California Press.

Carothers, T. 2002. The end of the transition paradigm. *Journal of Democracy* 13(1): 5–21.

Casper, G. 1995. *Fragile democracies: The legacies of authoritarian rule.* Pittsburgh, PA: University of Pittsburgh Press.

Collier, D., and S. Levitsky. 1997. Democracy with adjectives: Conceptual innovation in comparative research. *World Politics* 49(3): 430–451.

Collier, R. B., and D. Collier. 1991. Shaping the political Arena: Critical junctures, the labor movement, and regime dynamics in Latin America. Princeton, NJ: Princeton University Press.

Colombijn, F., and J. T. Lindblad, eds. 2002. Roots of violence in Indonesia: Contemporary violence in historical perspective. Leiden: KITLV Press.

Cribb, R, ed. 1990. The Indonesian killings of 1965–1966: Studies from Java and Bali. Melbourne: Centre of Southeast Asian Studies, Monash University.

Crouch, H. 1979. Patrimonialism and military rule in Indonesia. *World Politics* 31(4): 571–587.

Dahl, R. A. 1971. *Polyarchy: Participation and opposition.* New Haven, CT: Yale University Press.

Dahl, R. A. 1989. *Democracy and its critics.* New Haven, CT: Yale University Press.

Davidson, J. 2007. Politics-as-usual on trial: Regional anti-corruption campaigns in Indonesia. *Pacific Review* 20(1): 75–99.

Di Palma, G. 1990. *To craft democracies: An essay on democratic transitions.* Berkeley, CA: University of California Press.

Diamond, L. 1996. Is the third wave over? *Journal of Democracy* 7(3): 20–37.

———. 1997. *Consolidating the third wave democracies.* Baltimore: Johns Hopkins University Press.

———. 2002. Elections without democracy. *Journal of Democracy* 13(2): 21–36.

———. 2003. "Universal Democracy?" *Policy Review.* 119 (June and July): 1–25.

Diamond, L. and M. F. Plattner. eds. 2006. *Electoral Systems and Democracy.* Baltimore: Johns Hopkins University Press.

Dick, H. W. 1985. The rise of a middle class and the changing concept of equity in Indonesia: An interpretation. *Indonesia* 39 (April 1985): 71–92.

Draper, M. 2002. Justice as a building block of democracy in transitional societies: The case of Indonesia. *Colombia Journal of Transnational Law* 40(2): 391–418.

Eckardt, S. 2008. Political accountability, fiscal conditions and local government performance—cross-sectional evidence from Indonesia. *Public Administration and Development* 28(1): 1–17.

Emmerson, D. K. 2004. A year of voting dangerously. *The Journal of Democracy* 15(1): 94–108.

Erb, M., P. Sulistiyanto and C. Faucher. 2005. Regionalism in post-Suharto Indonesia. London and New York: RoutledgeCurzon.

Ethier, D., ed. 1990. *Democratic transition and consolidation in Southern Europe, Latin America and Southeast Asia.* Basingstoke, UK: Macmillan Press.

Feith, H. 1980. Repressive-developmentalist regimes in Asia: Old strengths, new vulnerabilities. *Prisma* 19 (December): 39–55.

Feith, H., and L. Castles. 1970. *Indonesian political thinking, 1945–1965.* Ithaca, NY: Cornell University Press.

Ferrazzi, G. 2000. Using the "F" word: Federalism in Indonesia's decentralization discourse. *Publuis—The Journal of Federalism* 30(2): 63–85.

Fitrani, F., B. Hofman, and K. Kaiser. 2005. Unity in diversity? The creation of new local governments in a decentralizing Indonesia. *Bulletin of Indonesian Economic Studies* 41(1): 57–79.

Ford, M. 2000. Continuity and change in Indonesian labour relations in the Habibie interregnum. *Asian Journal of Social Science* 28(2): 59–88.

Frank, A. G. 1967. *Capitalism and underdevelopment in Latin America: Historical studies of Brazil and Chile.* New York: Monthly Review Press.

Geddes, B. 1990. How the cases you choose affect the answers you get: Selection bias in comparative politics. *Political Analysis* 2: 131–150.

Geertz, C. 1960. *The religion of Java.* Chicago: Chicago University Press.

Gerschenkron, A. 1962. *Economic backwardness in historical perspective: A book of essays.* New York: Praeger.

Gramsci, A. 1971. *Selections from the prison notebooks of Antonio Gramsci.* Trans. Quintin Hoare and Geoffrey Nowell Smith, eds. London and New York: International Publishers.

Hadiz, V. 2003. Reorganizing political power in Indonesia: A reconsideration of so-called "Democratic Transitions." *Pacific Review* 16(4): 591–611.

Hainsworth, G., S. Turner, and D. Webster. 2007. Introduction: Indonesia's democratic struggle: Reformasi, *Otonomi* and *Participasi. Asia Pacific Viewpoint* 48(1): 41–46.

Hamayotsu, K. 2002. Islam and nation building in Southeast Asia: Malaysia and Indonesia in comparative perspective. *Pacific Affairs* 75(3): 353–375.

Heryanto, A. 1999. The years of living luxuriously: Identity politics of Indonesia's new rich. Culture and Privilege in Capitalist Asia. M. Pinches, ed., 159–187. New York: Routledge.

Hill, H. 1996. *The Indonesian economy since 1966: Southeast Asia's emerging giant.* Cambridge: Cambridge University Press.

———. 1999. *The Indonesian economy in crisis: Causes, consequences and lessons.* Sydney: Allen & Unwin.

Hill, H., and T. Shiraishi. 2007. Indonesia after the Asian crisis. *Asian Economic Policy Review* 2(1): 123–141.

Huntington, S.P. 1965. Political development and political decay. *World Politics* 17(3): 386–430.

———. 1968. *Political order in changing societies.* New Haven, CT: Yale University Press.

———. 1991. The third wave: Democratization in the late twentieth century. Norman: University of Oklahoma Press.

Johnson Tan, P. 2006. Indonesia seven years after Soeharto: Party system institutionalization in a new democracy. *Contemporary Southeast Asia* 28(1): 88–114.

Kadir, S. 1999. The Islamic factor in Indonesia's political transition. *Asian Journal of Political Science* 7(2): 21–44.

Karl, T. L. 1990. Dilemmas of democratization in Latin America. *Comparative Politics* 23(1): 1–23.

Karl, T. L., and P. C. Schmitter. 1991. Modes of transition in Latin America and Eastern Europe. *International Social Science Journal* 43(128): 269–284.

Kim, Y. C., R. W. Liddle, and S. Said. 2006. Political leadership and civilian supremacy in third wave democracies: Comparing South Korea and Indonesia. *Pacific Affairs* 79(2): 247–268.

King, D. Y. 2003. *Half-hearted reform: Electoral institutions and the struggle for democracy in Indonesia.* Westport, CT: Praeger.

Kingsbury, D. 2003. Diversity in unity. *Autonomy and disintegration in Indonesia.* D. Kingsbury and H. Aveling, eds., 99–114. London: RoutledgeCurzon.

Kirchheimer, O. 1965. Confining conditions and revolutionary breakthroughs. *American Political Science Review* 59(4): 964–974.

Koentjaraningrat, R. M. 1985. *Javanese culture.* Singapore, Oxford, and New York: Oxford University Press.

Lane, M. 1999. Mass politics and political change in Indonesia. Reformasi: *Crisis and change in Indonesia.* A. Budiman, B. Hatley, and D. Kingsbury, eds., 239–251. Melbourne: Monash Asia Institute.

Liddle, R. W. 1992. Indonesia's democratic past and future. *Comparative Politics* 24(2): 443–462.

———. 1996. The Islamic turn in Indonesia. *The Journal of Asian Studies* 55(3): 613–634.

Liddle, R. W., and S. Mujani. 2006. Indonesia in 2005: A new multiparty presidential democracy. *Asian Survey* 46(1): 132–139.

Linz, J. J. 1990. Transitions to democracy. *Washington Monthly* 2(2): 12–34.

Linz, J. J., and A. C. Stepan. 1978. *The breakdown of democratic regimes.* Baltimore: Johns Hopkins University Press.

————. 1996. *Problems of democratic transition and consolidation: Southern Europe, South America and post-communist Europe.* Baltimore: Johns Hopkins University Press.

Lipset, S. M. 1959. Some social requisites of democracy: Economic development and political legitimacy. *American Political Science Review* **53**(1): 69–105.

MacIntyre, A. 1991. *Business and politics in Indonesia.* Sydney: Allen & Unwin.

————. 2000. Funny money: Fiscal policy, rent seeking and economic performance in Indonesia. *Rent Seeking in Southeast Asia.* K. S. Jomo and M. Khan, eds., 248–273. Cambridge: Cambridge University Press.

Mackie, J. A. C. 1990. Property and power in Indonesia. Money and the middle class. *The Politics of the Middle Class in Indonesia.* R. Tanter and K. Young, eds., 71–95 and 96–122. Victoria, Australia: Aristoc Press.

Mahoney J. 2000. Path dependence in historical sociology. *Theory and Society* **29**(4): 507–548.

Mainwaring, S., G. O'Donnell and Valenzuela, J.S. eds. 1992. *Issues in democratic consolidation: The new South American democracies in comparative perspective.* South Bend, IN: University of Notre Dame Press.

Malley, M. (2002a). Indonesia in 2001: Restoring stability in Jakarta. *Asian Survey* **42**(1): 124–132.

Mamdani, M. 1996. *Citizen and subject: contemporary Africa and the legacy of late colonialism.* Princeton, NJ: Princeton University Press.

Markoff, J. 1997. Really existing democracy: Learning from Latin America in the late 1990s. *New Left Review* (223): 48–68.

Mas'oed, M. 1989. *Ekonomi dan struktur politik Orde Baru, 1966–1971.* Jakarta: Lembaga Penelititan Pendidikan dan Penerangan Ekonomi dan Sosial.

McCulloch, L. 2003. *Trifungsi*: The role of the Indonesian military in business. *The military as economic actor—soldiers in business.* J. Brommelhorster and W. C. Paes, eds. London: Palgrave Macmillan: 94–124.

McFaul, M. 2002. The fourth wave of democracy and dictatorship: Non-cooperative transitions in the post-communist world. *World Politics* **54**(2): 212–244.

Mietzner, M. 2001. Abdurrahman's Indonesia: Political conflict and institutional crisis. *Indonesia Today: Challenges of History.* L. Grayson and S. Smith, eds., 29–44. Singapore: Institute of Southeast Asian Studies.

Montero, A. 1998. Review essay: Assessing the third wave democracies. *Journal of Inter-American Studies and World Affairs* **40**(2): 119–120.

Moore, B. 1966. *Social origins of dictatorship and democracy: Lord and peasant in the making of the modern world.* Boston: Beacon.

Mouzelis, N. 1986. *Politics of the semi-periphery.* London: Macmillan Publishers.

Mulder, N. 1998. *Mysticism in Java: Ideology in Indonesia.* Amsterdam: Pepin.

Munck, G. 1993. Between theory and history and beyond traditional area studies: A new comparative perspective on Latin America. *Comparative Politics* **25**(4): 475–498.

Munck, G. 1994. Democratic transitions in comparative perspective. *Comparative Politics* **26**(3): 355–375.

North, D. C. 1990. *Institutions, Institutional change and economic performance.* Cambridge: Cambridge University Press.

O'Donnell, G. 1973. *Modernisation and bureaucratic authoritarianism.* Berkeley, CA: Institute of International Studies.

O'Donnell, G. 1996. Illusions about consolidation. *Journal of Democracy* **7**(2): 34–51.

O'Donnell, G., P. Schmitter, and L. Whitehead, eds. 1986. *Transitions from authoritarian rule* (Four Volumes). Baltimore: Johns Hopkins University Press.

Ottoway, M. 2003. *Democracy challenged: The rise of semi-authoritarianism.* Washington, DC: Carnegie Foundation.

Panebianco, A. 1988. *Political parties: Organization and power.* Cambridge / New York: Cambridge University Press.

Philpott, S. 2000. Rethinking Indonesia: Postcolonial theory, authoritarianism and identity. New York: St. Martin's Press; Basingstoke, UK: Macmillan.

Pierson, P. 2000. Not just what, but when: Timing and sequence in political processes. *Studies in American Political Development* **14**(2): 72–92.

Pirandello, L. [1921] 1952. *Six characters in search of an author.* Trans. E. Bentley. New York: E.P Dutton.

Poulantzas, N. 1976. *The crisis of the dictatorships: Portugal, Greece, Spain.* London: New Left Books and Humanities Press.

Pridham, G. 1990. Political actors, linkages and interactions: Democratic consolidation in Southern Europe. *West European Politics* **13**(4): 103–117.

Pridham, G. 2000. *The dynamics of democratization: A comparative approach.* London and New York: Continuum.

Przeworski, A. 1991. *Democracy and the market: Political and economic reforms in Eastern Europe and Latin America*. Cambridge: Cambridge University Press.

Przeworski, A., and F. Limongi. 1993. Political regimes and economic growth. *Journal of Economic Perspectives*. 7(1): 51–70.

———. 1997. Modernization: Theories and facts. *World Politics*. 49(2): 155–183.

Przeworski, A., M. Alvarez, A. Cheibub, and F. Limongi. 2000. *Democracy and development: Political institutions and well-being in the world, 1950–1990*. New York: Cambridge University Press.

Pye, L. W., and M. W. Pye. 1985. *Asian power and politics: The cultural dimensions of authority*. Cambridge, MA: Belknap Press.

Rasyid, M. R. 2000. Political reform in Indonesia: Taking the democratic path. *The political dimensions of the Asian crisis*. U. Johannen, J. Rudolph, and J. Gomez, eds., 151–156. Singapore: Institute of Southeast Asian Studies.

Remmer, K. 1982. Bureaucratic authoritarianism revisited. *Latin American Research Review* 17: 3–36.

Robison, R. 1986. *Indonesia: The rise of capital*. Canberra: Allen & Unwin.

Robison, R., and V. Hadiz. 2004. Reorganizing power in Indonesia: The politics of oligarchy in an age of markets. London: RoutledgeCurzon.

Rodan, G. ed. 1996. *Political oppositions in industrializing Asia*. London and New York: Routledge.

Rostow, W. W. 1960. *The stages of economic growth: a non-communist manifesto*. Cambridge: Cambridge University Press.

Rueschemeyer, D., E. Stephens, and D. Stephens. 1992. *Capitalist development and democracy*. Chicago: Chicago University Press.

Rustow, D. (1970). Transitions to Democracy: Toward a Dynamic Model. *Comparative Politics* 2(3): 337–363.

Schedler, A. 1998. What is democratic consolidation? *Journal of Democracy* 9(2): 91–107.

Schiller, J., and B. Martin-Schiller, eds. 1997. *Imagining Indonesia: Cultural politics and political culture*. Athens: Ohio University Press.

Schmitter, P. C. 1992. The consolidation of democracy and representation of social groups. *American Behavioral Scientist* 35(4–5): 422–449.

Schmitter, P. C., and T. L. Karl. 1994. The conceptual travels of transitologists and consolidologists: How far to the East should they attempt. *Slavic Review* 53(1): 173–185.

Schulte Nordholt, H. 2003. Renegotiating boundaries: Access, agency and identity in post-Suharto Indonesia. *Bijdragen tot de Taal-Land-en Volkenkunde* 159(4): 550–589.

Schwartz, A. 1994. *A nation in waiting: Indonesia in the 1990s.* Sydney and Boulder, CO: Westview Press.

Share, D. 1987. Transitions to democracy and transitions through transaction. *Comparative Political Studies* 19(4): 525–547.

Shin, D. C. 1994. On the third wave of democratisation: A synthesis and evaluation of recent theory and research. *World Politics* 47: 135–170.

Singh, B. 2000. Civil-military relations in democratising Indonesia: Change amidst continuity. *Armed Forces and Society* 26(4): 184–216.

Skocpol, T. 1979. *States and social revolutions: A comparative analysis of France, Russia and China.* Cambridge: Cambridge University Press.

Slater, D. 2006. The ironies of instability in Indonesia. *Social Analysis* 50(1): 208–213.

Smith, A. 2001. Indonesia: Transforming the Leviathian. Government and politics in Southeast Asia. J. Funston, ed., 74–117. London: Zed Books Limited.

Sukma, R. 2003. Conflict management in post-authoritarian Indonesia. *Autonomy and disintegration in Indonesia.* D. Kingsbury and H. Aveling, eds., 64–74. London: RoutledgeCurzon.

Tiwon, S. 2000. From East Timor to Aceh: The disintegration of Indonesia. *Bulletin of Concerned Asian Scholars* 32(1–2): 97–104.

Toer, P. A. [1975] 1996. This earth of mankind (Buru Quartet). Trans. M. Lane. London: Penguin Books.

Tomsa, D. 2008. *Party politics and democratization in Indonesia: Golkar in the post-Suharto era.* London and New York: Routledge.

Tornquist, O. 2000. Dynamics of Indonesian democracy. *Third World Quarterly* 21(3): 383–423.

Turner, M., O. Podger, M. Samardjono, and W. K. Tirthayasa. 2003. *Decentralisation in Indonesia: Redesigning the state.* Canberra: Asia Pacific Press.

Uhlin, A. 1997. *Indonesia and the "Third Wave of Democratization": The Indonesian pro-democracy movement in a changing world.* New York: St. Martin's Press.

Wallerstien, I. 1979. *The capitalist world-economy.* Cambridge: Cambridge University Press.

Webber. D. 2006. A consolidated patrimonial democracy? Democratization in post-Suharto Indonesia. *Democratization* 13(3): 396–420.

Weber, M. [1924] 1962. *Basic concepts in Sociology*. Trans. H. P. Sechers. New York: The Citadel Press.

Whitehead, L. 2002. *Democratization: Theory and experience*. Oxford: Oxford University Press.

Zakaria, F. 1997. The rise of illiberal democracy. *Foreign Affairs* 76(6) (November/December): 22–43.

NEWSPAPERS AND NEWS PERIODICALS

Harinowo, C. 2008. Economic growth: The rise of the Indonesian middle class. *Jakarta Post*. Jakarta, September 16.

McBride, E. 2004. Survey: Indonesia. The Economist. London, December 9.

MacDonald, H. 2007. Increasingly sophisticated Yudhoyono will leave an impressive record. *Sydney Morning Herald*. September 15.

Mulia, E. 2008. Prevention crucial to combat corruption. *Jakarta Post*. Jakarta, March 6.

Pabottingi, M. 2002. In Golkar's grip. *Tempo*. Jakarta, January 6.

REPORTS AND SURVEYS

Asia Foundation. 2003. Democracy in Indonesia: A survey of the Indonesian electorate, 1–298. Washington, DC: Asia Foundation.

NDI. 1999. The 1999 presidential election and post election development in Indonesia. A post election assessment report, November 28. Washington, DC: National Democratic Institute.

———. 2003a. Law on the general election of the president and vice-president—Passed by DPR on 8 July 2003: A short guide. October 3. Washington, DC: National Democratic Institute.

———. 2003b. Law on the structure and the composition of the MPR, DPR, DPD and DPRDs—Passed by the DPR on 9 July 2003: A short guide, October 9, 2003. National Democratic Institute.

UNDP. 1997. Concepts of governance and sustainable human development, 1–20. New York: United Nations Development Programme.

FURTHER READING

Abuza, Z. 2002. Tentacles of terror: Al Qaeda's Southeast Asian network. *Contemporary Southeast Asia* 24(3): 427–465.

Alagappa, M., ed. 1995. Political legitimacy in Southeast Asia. *Contemporary issues in Asia and the Pacific*. Stanford: Stanford University Press.

Almond, G. A., and S. Verba. 1963. *The civic culture: Political attitudes and democracy in five nations.* Princeton, NJ: Princeton University Press.

Anderson, B., and A. Kahin. eds. 1982. *Interpreting Indonesian politics: Thirteen contributions to the debate.* Ithaca, NY: Cornell Modern Indonesia Project, Southeast Asia Program, Cornell University.

Anek, L. 1997. *Democratization in Southeast and East Asia.* New York: St. Martin's Press; Singapore: Institute of Southeast Asian Studies.

Antlov, H. 2003a. Not enough politics! Power, participation and the new democratic polity in Indonesia. *Local power and politics in Indonesia: Decentralisation and democratisation.* E. Aspinall and G. Fealy, eds., 72–86. Singapore: Institute of Southeast Asian Studies.

Anwar, D. F. 1999. The Habibie presidency. *Post Soeharto: Renewal or chaos?* G. Forrester ed. Bathurst, UK: Crawford House.

Anwar, D. F. 2001. Indonesia's transition to democracy: Challenges and prospects. *Indonesia: The uncertain transition.* D. Kingsbury and A. Budiman, eds., 3–16. Adelaide: Crawford House.

Aspinall, E., and M. Berger. 2001. The break-up of Indonesia? Nationalisms after decolonisation and the limits of the nation-state in post-Cold war Southeast Asia. *Third World Quarterly* 22(6): 1003–1024.

Aspinall, E., H. Feith, and G. van Klinken, eds. 1999. *The last days of President Suharto.* Melbourne: Monash Asia Institute.

Baker, R., ed. 1999. *Indonesia: The challenge of change.* Singapore: Institute of Southeast Asian Studies.

Bakti, A. F., ed. 2000. *Good governance and conflict resolution in Indonesia: From authoritarian government to civil society.* Jakarta: Logos.

Bandoro, B. 2001. Indonesia: A "broken-backed" state? *Indonesian Quarterly* 29(4): 333–337.

Bandoro, B. 2002. War against terror: Lessons from Indonesia. *Indonesian Quarterly* 30(3): 234–236.

Barton, G. 2000. View from the top, parliament, the constitution, and the future, as seen from the presidential palace. *Inside Indonesia* 8(4): 22–56.

———. 2002a. *Abdurrahmin Wahid: Muslim democrat, Indonesian president.* Sydney: UNSW Press.

Bell, G. 2003. Indonesia: The regional autonomy, two years later. *Southeast Asian Affairs* 3(2): 117–131.

Ben-Doi, G. 1975. Institutionalisation and political development: A conceptual and theoretical analysis. *Comparative Studies in History and Society* 17: 309–325.

Bertrand, J. 1996. False starts, succession crises and regime transition: Flirting with openness in Indonesia. *Pacific Affairs* 69(3): 319–340.

Bertrand, J. 1997. Business as usual in Suharto's Indonesia. *Asian Survey* 37(5): 44–56.

Blackburn, S., ed. 1999. *Pemilu: The 1999 Indonesian election.* Melbourne: Monash Asia Institute.

Booth, A., ed. 1992. *The oil boom and after: Indonesian economic policy and performance in the Soeharto era.* Singapore: Oxford University Press.

Boudrea, V. 1999. Diffusing democracy? People power in Indonesia and the Phillipines. *Bulletin of Concerned Asian Scholars* 31(4): 3–18.

Bourchier, D. 1994. The 1950s in New Order ideology and politics. *Democracy in Indonesia 1950s and 1990s.* D. Bourchier and J. Legge, eds., 50–62. Melbourne: Centre of Southeast Asian Studies, Monash University.

———. 1998. How the New Order collapsed. *Inside Indonesia* 55: 5–6.

———. 1999. Magic memos, collusion and judges with attitude. *Law, capitalism and power in Asia: The rule of law and legal institutions.* K. Jayasuriya, ed., 233–252. London: Routledge.

———. 2001. Conservative political ideology in Indonesia: A fourth wave? *Indonesia today: Challenges of history.* L. Grayson and S. Smith, eds., 112–125. Singapore: Institute of Southeast Asian Studies.

Brass, P. R. 1991. *Ethnicity and nationalism: Theory and comparison.* New Delhi and Newbury Park, CA: Sage Publications.

———. 1997. *Theft of an idol: Text and context in the representation of collective violence.* Princeton, NJ: Princeton University Press.

Brown, D. 1994. *The state and ethnic politics in Southeast Asia.* London: Routledge.

Browne, S. J. 1998. Irian Jaya: 30 years of Indonesian control, 1–32. Working Papers. Melbourne: Centre for Southeast Asian Studies, Monash University.

Budiardjo, C. 2001. *State terror in Indonesia, past and present,* 1–8. London: Tapol.

Budiman, A., ed. 1990. *State and civil society in Indonesia.* Melbourne: Centre of Southeast Asian Studies, Monash University.

Budiman, A., B. Hatley, and D. Kingsbury, eds. 1999. *Reformasi: Crisis and change in Indonesia.* Melbourne: Centre of Southeast Asian Studies, Monash University.

Bulkin, F. 1983. *State and society: Indonesian society under the New Order 1966–1978.* Washington, DC: University of Washington.

Bunce, V. 1995. Should transitologists be grounded? *Slavic Review* 54(1): 111–127.

Bunce, V., and M. Csanadi. 1993. Uncertainty in transition: Post-communism in Hungary. *Eastern European Politics and Society* 7: 32–50.

Caldeira, T., and J. Holston. 1999. Democracy and violence in Brazil. *Comparative Studies in Society and History* 41(4): 691–729.

Cammack, P. 1985. Democratisation: A review of the issues. *Bulletin of Latin American Research* 4(2): 39–46.

Case, W. F. 1996. Can the "halfway house" stand? Semi-democracy and elite theory in three Southeast Asian Countries. *Comparative Politics* 28(4): 437–464.

———. 2000. Revisiting elites, transitions, and founding elections: An unexpected caller from Indonesia. *Democratization* 7(4): 51–80.

Casper, G. 1996. Negotiating democracy: Transitions from authoritarian rule. Pittsburgh, PA: University of Pittsburgh Press.

Chehabi, H., and J. J. Linz, eds. 1998. *Sultanistic regimes.* Baltimore: Johns Hopkins University Press.

Collier, D. 1979. *The new authoritarianism in Latin America.* Princeton, NJ: Princeton University Press.

Collier, D., and J. Mahoney. 1996. Insights and pitfalls: Selection bias in qualitative research. *World Politics* 49(1): 56–91.

Colongon, A. 2003. What is happening on the ground? The progress of decentralisation. *Local power and politics in Indonesia: Decentralisation and democratisation.* E. Aspinall and G. Fealy, eds., 87–101. Singapore: Institute of Southeast Asian Studies.

Considine, M. 1994. *Public policy: A critical approach.* Melbourne: Macmillan Education Australia.

Cribb, R. 1999a. Nation: Making Indonesia. *Indonesia beyond Suharto: Polity, economy, society transition.* D. K. Emmerson, ed., 3–38. Armonk, NY: ME Sharpe.

———. 1999b. Not the next Yugoslavia: Prospects for the disintegration of Indonesia. *Australian Journal of International Affairs* 53(2): 169–178.

Crouch, H. 1978. *The army and politics in Indonesia.* Ithaca, NY: Cornell University Press.

———. 2000. *Indonesia: Democratization and the threat of disintegration,* 115–133. Singapore: Institute of Southeast Asian Studies.

———. 2003. Political update 2002: Megawati's holding operation. *Local power and politics in Indonesia.* E. Aspinall and G. Fealy. eds., 15–34. Singapore: Institute of Southeast Asian Studies.

Dahl, R. A. 1956. *A preface to democratic theory.* Chicago: University of Chicago Press.

Darmaputera, D. 1988. *Pancasila and the search for identity and modernity in Indonesian society.* Leiden: E. J. Brill.

Davidson, J. 2003. The politics of violence on an Indonesian periphery. *Southeast Asian Research* 11(1): 59–89. Diamond, L. 1992. *The democratic revolution: Struggles for freedom and pluralism in the developing world.* New York: Freedom House.

Diamond, L. 1993. *Political culture and democracy in developing countries.* Boulder, CO: Lynne Rienner Publishers.

Diederich, M. 2002. A closer look at "Dakwah" and politics in Indonesia: The Partai Keadilan. *Archipel* 64: 20–39.

Duncan, C. 2007. Mixed outcomes: The impact of regional autonomy and decentralization on indigenous ethnic minorities in Indonesia. *Development and Change* 38(4): 711–733.

Eklof, S. 1999. *Indonesian politics in crisis: The long fall of Suharto* 1996–1998. Copenhagen: Nordic Institute of Asian Studies.

———. 2002. Politics, business and democratization. *Political Business in East Asia.* E. Gomez, ed., 216–249. London: Routledge.

Emmerson, D. K. 1995. Region and recalcitrance: Rethinking democracy through Southeast Asia. *The Pacific Review* 8(2): 223–248.

———. 1999. *Indonesia beyond Suharto: Polity, economy, society, transition.* Armonk, NY: ME Sharpe.

Erawan, I. K. P. 1999. Political reform and regional politics in Indonesia. *Asian Survey* 39(4): 588–612.

Falaakh, M. F. 1999. Islam and the current transition to democracy in Indonesia. Reformasi: *Crisis and change in Indonesia.* A. Budiman, B. Hatley, and D. Kingsbury, eds., 201–212. Melbourne: Centre for Southeast Asian Studies, Monash University.

———. 2001. Nahdlatul Ulama and civil society in Indonesia. *Islam and civil society in Southeast Asia.* M. Nakamura, S. Siddique, and O. Bajunid, eds. Singapore: Institute of Southeast Asian Studies.

Fanany, I. 2003. The first year of local autonomy: The case of West Sumatra. *Autonomy and Disintegration in Indonesia.* D. Kingsbury and H. Aveling, eds., 177–188. London: RoutledgeCurzon.

Forrester, G. ed. 1999. Post-Soeharto Indonesia: Renewal or chaos. Bathurst, Australia: Crawford House Publishing.

Fukuyama, F. 1992. *The end of history and the last man.* New York: Free Press.

Geddes, B. 1994. *Politician's dilemma: Building state capacity in Latin America.* Berkeley, CA: University of California Press.

———. 1999. What do we know about democratization after twenty years? *Annual Review of Political Science* 2: 115–144.

Geertz, H. 1961. *The Javanese family: A study of kinship and socialization.* New York: Free Press of Glencoe.

Gellner, E. 1983. *Nations and nationalism.* Oxford: Blackwell.

Gerth, H. H., and C. Wright Mills, eds. 1958. From Max Weber: Essays in sociology. London: Routledge and Kegan Paul.

Ghohal, B. 2000. Students and politics in Indonesia: The role of KAMI. *Indonesia: Government and Politics.* V. Grover, ed., 174–187. New Delhi: Deep Publications.

Gill, G. 2000. The dynamics of democratization: Elites, civil society and the transitional process. Basingstoke, UK: Macmillan Press.

Gouda, F. 2000. Mimicry and projection in the colonial encounter: The Dutch East Indies/Indonesia as experimental laboratory, 1900–1942. *Journal of Colonialism and Colonial History* 1(2): 1–20.

Hadiz, V. 2004. The rise of neo-third worldism? The Indonesian trajectory and the consolidation of illiberal democracy. *Third World Quarterly* 25(1): 55–71.

Hadiz, V., and R. Robison. 2005. Neo-liberal reforms and illiberal consolidations: The Indonesian paradox. *Journal of Development Studies* 41(2): 220–241.

Haggard, S., and R. Kaufman, eds. 1995 *The political economy of democratic transitions.* Princeton, NJ: Princeton University Press.

———. 1997. The political economy of democratic transitions. *Comparative Politics* 29(3): 263–283.

Halliday, F. 2003. *Islam and the myth of confrontation: Religion and politics in the Middle East.* London: I. B. Tauris.

Hasan, N. 2002. Faith and politics: The rise of Laskar Jihad in the era of transition in Indonesia. *Indonesian Quarterly* 73(2): 4–18.

Hefner, R. 1997a. Islam in an era of nation-states: Politics and religious renewal in Muslim Southeast Asia. *Islam in an era of nation-states.* R. Hefner and P. Horvatich, eds., 3–42. Honolulu: University of Hawaii Press.

———. 2000. *Civil Islam: Muslims and democratization in Indonesia.* Princeton, NJ: Princeton University Press.

———. 2001. *Politics of multiculturalism: Pluralism and citizenship in Malaysia, Singapore and Indonesia.* Honolulu: University of Hawaii Press.

———. 2002. Civil Islam, democratization, and violence in Indonesia: A comment. *Review of Indonesia and Malaysian Affairs* 36(1): 67–75.

Hefner, R and P. Horvatich, eds. 1997. *Islam in an era of nation-states: Politics and religions renewal in Muslim Southeast Asia.* Honolulu: University of Hawaii Press.

Helmke, G., and S. Levitsky. 2006. *Informal institutions and democracy: Lessons from Latin America.* Baltimore: Johns Hopkins University Press.

Heryanto, A. 2003. Public intellectuals, media, and democratization. *Challenging authoritarianism in Southeast Asia: Comparing Indonesia and Malaysia*. A. Heryanto and S. Mandal, eds., 25–59. New York: RoutledgeCurzon.

Hidayat, S. 1999. Decentralised politics in a centralised political system: A study of local state power in West Java and West Sumatra in New Order Indonesia. *Masyarakat Indonesia* 25(1): 151–166.

Hill, H. 1994. Indonesia's New Order: The dynamics of socio-economic transformation. Honolulu: University of Hawaii Press.

Hoey, B. 2003. Nationalism and Indonesia. *Ethnology* 42(2): 110–126.

Honna, J. 2003. *Military politics and democratization in Indonesia*. London: RoutledgeCurzon.

Hosen, N. 2003. Fatwa and politics in Indonesia. *Shari'a and Politics in modern Indonesia*. A. Salim and A. Azra, eds., 168–180. Singapore: Institute of Southeast Asian Studies.

Hyman, G. 2002. Tilting at straw men. *Journal of Democracy* 13(3): 26–32.

Ismanto, I., and T. Legowo 1999. Post-election politics and Indonesia's new regime reformation. *Indonesian Quarterly* 27(4): 307–315.

Jones, D. M. 1998. Democratization, civil society and illiberal middle class culture in Pacific Asia. *Comparative Politics* 30(2): 147–169.

Khan, J., and F. Formosa. 2002. The problem of crony capitalism: Modernity and the encounter with the perverse. *Thesis Eleven* 69(1): 47–66.

Kingsbury, D. 1999. The political resurgence of Tentara Nasional Indonesia. *Pemuli: The 1999 Indonesian Election*. S. Blackburn, ed., 50–72. Melbourne: Monash Asia Institute.

———. 2000. The reform of the Indonesian armed forces. *Contemporary Southeast Asia* 22(2): 302–330.

———. 2003. *Power politics and the Indonesian military*. London: RoutledgeCurzon.

Kitschelt, H. 1992. Political regime change: Structure and process-driven explanations? *American Political Science Review* 86(4): 1028–1034.

———. 1993. Comparative historical research and rational choice theory. The case of transitions to democracy. *Theory and Society* 22(3): 413–427.

Kohar, E. 2001. Democratic consolidation in Indonesia: Hopes and reality. *Indonesian Quarterly* 29(1): 43–55.

Lee, T. 2000. The nature and future of civil-military relations in Indonesia. *Asian Survey* 40: 4–22.

Leftwich, A., ed. 1996. Democracy and development: Theory and practice. Cambridge, MA: Polity Press.

Legowo, T. 2002. Indonesia's political reform: Still a long way to go. *Indonesian Quarterly* 30(2): 117–124.

Levitsky, S., and Way, L. 2005 International linkage and democratization. *Journal of Democracy* 16(3): 20–34.

Liddle, R. W. 1999. Indonesia's democratic opening. *Government and Opposition* 34(1): 94–116.

———. 2000. Indonesia in 1999. *Asian Survey* 40(1): 32–38.

———. 2001. Indonesia in 2000: A shaky start for democracy. *Asian Survey* 41(1): 208–224.

Lijphart, A. 1975. The comparable-case strategy in comparative research. *Comparative Political Studies* 8(2): 158–175.

Lindsay, J. 2002. Television, orality and performance: Indonesia's 1999 elections. *Archipel* 64: 323–336.

Linton, S. 2004. Unravelling the first three trials at Indonesia's ad hoc court for human rights violations in East Timor. *Leiden Journal for International Law* 17: 303–361.

Linz, J. J., and A. Valenzuela, eds. 1994. *Comparative perspectives.* Baltimore: Johns Hopkins University Press.

Lipset, S. M. 1963. *Political man.* London: Mercury Books.

Loveard, K. 1999. *Suharto: Indonesia's last sultan.* Singapore: Institute of Asian Studies.

Mackie, J. A. C. 1994. Inevitable or avoidable? Interpretations of the collapse of parliamentary democracy. *Democracy in Indonesia: 1950s and 1990s.* D. Bourchier and J. D. Legge, eds., 26–38. Melbourne: Centre for Southeast Asian Studies.

Malley, M. (2002b). Political centralization and social conflict. *Ethnic conflict: Religion, identity and politics.* S. Giannakos, ed. Athens: Ohio University Press: 170–189.

Manning, C., and P. van Diermen, eds. 2000. *Indonesia in transition: Social aspects of Reformasi and crisis.* Singapore: Institute of Southeast Asian Studies.

Markoff, J. 1996. *Waves of democracy: Social movements and political change.* Thousand Oaks, CA: Pine Forge Press.

McLeod, R. H. 2000. Soeharto's Indonesia: A better class of corruption. *Agenda* 7(2): 99–112.

McVey, R. 1983. Faith as the outsider: Islam in Indonesian politics. *Islam in the political process.* J. Piscatori, ed. Cambridge: Cambridge University Press.

Mietzner, M. 1999a. From Soeharto to Habibie: The Indonesian Armed Forces and political Islam during the transition. *Post-Soeharto Indonesia: renewal or chaos?* G. Forrester, ed., 65–104. Bathurst, Australia: Crawford House Publishing.

————. 1999b. Nationalism and Islamic politics: Political Islam in the post-Suharto era. *Reformasi: Crisis and change in Indonesia.* A. Budiman, B. Hatley, and D. Kingsbury, eds., 173–200. Melbourne: Monash Asia Institute.

————. 1999c. Nahdlatul Ulama and the 1999 general election in Indonesia. *Pemilu: The 1999 Indonesian election.* S. Blackburn, ed., 73–85. Melbourne: Monash Asia Institute.

————. 2000. The 1999 general session: Wahid, Megawati and the fight for the presidency. *Indonesia in transition: Social aspects of reformasi and crisis,* 47–62. Singapore: Institute of Southeast Asian Studies.

Morfit, M. 1981. Pancasila: The Indonesian state ideology according to the New Order government. *Asian Survey* 21(8): 838–851.

Munck, G. 2001a. Game theory and comparative politics—new Perspectives and old concerns. *World Politics* 53(1): 173–204.

————. 2001b. The regime question—Theory building in democracy studies. *World Politics* 54(1): 119–144.

Munck, G., and C. S. Leff. 1997. Modes of transition and democratization: South America and Eastern Europe in Comparative Perspective. *Comparative Politics* 29(3): 343–362.

Nasution, A. 1998. The meltdown of the Indonesian economy in 1997–1998: Causes and responses. *The Seoul Journal of Economics* 11(4): 447–482.

————. 2001. Some notes on the electoral reform in Indonesia. Crafting Indonesian democracy. R. W. Liddle, ed., 133–136. Bandung: Indonesian Institute of Science.

Newland, L. 2000. Under the banner of Islam: Mobilising religious identities in West Java. *The Australian Journal of Anthropology* 11(2): 199–223.

Nishihara, M. 1972. Golkar and the Indonesia elections of 1971. *Cornell Modern Indonesia Project No. 56,* 1–57. Ithaca, NY.

O'Donnell, G. 1994. Delegative democracy. *Journal of Democracy* 5(1): 55–59.

O'Rourke, K. 2002. *Reformasi: The struggle for power in post-Soeharto Indonesia.* Sydney: Allen & Unwin.

Perwita, A. 2001. Political Islam and the use of societal approach in Indonesia's foreign policy. *Indonesian Quarterly* 29(4): 374–380.

Pierson, P. 2000. Increasing returns, path dependence, and the study of politics. *American Political Science Review* 94(2): 251–267.

Porter, D. 2002. Citizen participation through mobilisation and the rise of political Islam in Indonesia. *The Pacific Review* 15(2): 201–224.

Pridham, G., ed. 1991. *Encouraging democracy: The international context of regime transition in Southern Europe.* Leicester, UK: Leicester University Press.

————. 1991a. *Securing democracy: Political parties and democratic con-solidation in Southern Europe.* London: Routledge.

Przeworski, A. 1985. *Capitalism and social democracy.* Cambridge: Cambridge University Press.

————, ed. 2000. *Democracy and development. Cambridge studies in the theory of democracy.* Cambridge: Cambridge University Press.

Pye, L. W. 1990. Political science and the crisis of authoritarianism. *American Political Science Review* **84**: 3–19.

Ramage, D. 1995. *Politics in Indonesia: Democracy, Islam and the ideology of tolerance.* London: Routledge.

Rasyid, M. R. 2003. Regional autonomy and local politics. *Local power and politics in Indonesia: Decentralisation and democratisation.* E. Aspinall and G. Fealy, eds., 63–71. Singapore: Institute of South-east Asian Studies.

Reid, A., ed. 1993. *The making of an Islamic political discourse in Southeast Asia.* Melbourne: Monash University Press.

Remmer, K. 1995. New theoretical perspectives on democratisation. *Comparative Politics* **28**(1): 103–124.

Riddell, P. 2002. Diverse voices of political Islam in post-Suharto Indonesia. *Islam and Christian-Muslim Relations* **13**(1): 65–84.

Riggs, F. W. 1966. *Thailand: The modernisation of a bureaucratic polity.* Honolulu: East-West Centre Press.

Rodan, G., K. Hewison and R. Robison, eds. 2001. *The political economy of Southeast Asia: Conflicts, crises and change.* Melbourne: Oxford University Press.

Rueschemeyer, D., E. Stephens, and D. Stephens. (1997). The paradoxes of contemporary democracy. *Comparative Politics* **29**(3): 323–341.

Said, E. W. 1978. *Orientalism.* London: Routledge & Kegan Paul.

Sartori, G. 1970. Concept misinformation in comparative politics. *American Political Science Review* **64**: 1033–1053.

Sartori, G. 1973. *Democratic theory.* Westport, CT: Greenwood Press.

Sartori, G. 1987. *The theory of democracy revisited.* Chatham, NJ: Chatham House Publishers.

Schedler, A., ed. 2006. *Electoral authoritarianism: The dynamics of unfree competition.* Boulder, CO, and London: Lynne Rienner.

Schmittter, P. and T. L. Karl. 1994. Dangers and dilemmas of democracy. *Journal of Democracy* **5**(1): 57–74.

Schneider, B. 1995. Democratic consolidations: Some broad comparisons and sweeping arguments. *Latin American Research Review* **30**: 215–234.

Schulte Nordholt, N. 2001. Indonesia, a nation-state in search of identity and structure. *Bijdragen tot de Taal-Land-en Volkenkunde* **157**(4): 881–901.

———. 2002. A genealogy of violence. Roots of violence in Indonesia: Contemporary violence in historical perspective. F. Colombijn and J. T. Lindblad, eds., 33–61. Leiden: KLTV Press.

Schumpeter, J. A. 1943. *Capitalism, socialism and democracy.* London: Allen & Unwin.

Schwartz, A. 1999. *A nation in waiting: Indonesia's search for stability.* Sydney: Allen & Unwin.

Sebastian, L. C. 2004. The paradox of Indonesian democracy. *Contemporary Southeast Asia* 26(2): 256–277.

Shapiro, M. J. 1981. *Language and political understanding: The politics of discursive practices.* New Haven, CT: Yale University Press.

Sidel, J. 1999. Capital, coercion, and crime: Bossism in the Philippines. Stanford, CA: Stanford University Press.

Simanjuntak, M. 1994. *Pandanang negara integralistik: Sumber, unsur dan riwayantnya dalam persiapan UUD 1945* [The view of the integralist state: Sources, elements and its history in the preparation of the 1945 constitution]. Jakarta: Pustaka Utama Grafiti.

Skocpol, T. ed. 1998. Democracy, revolution, and history. Ithaca, NY: Cornell University Press.

Stepan, A. C. 1997. Democratic opposition and democratisation theory. *Government and Opposition* 36(1): 657–673.

Subekti, V. 2001. Electoral reform as prerequisite to create democratization in Indonesia. Crafting Indonesian democracy. R. W. Liddle, ed. Bandung: Indonesian Institute of Science.

Sumartana, T. 1999. Measuring the significance of religious political parties and pluralist parties in the 1999 general election in Indonesia. *Inter-Religious Bulletin* 36: 58–67.

Suryadinata, L. 2002. *Elections and politics in Indonesia.* Singapore: Institute of Southeast Asian Studies.

Suryadinata, L., E. Arifin, and A. Ananta, eds. 2003. Indonesia's population: Ethnicity and religion in a changing political landscape. Singapore: Institute of Southeast Asian Studies.

Tornquist, O. 2002. What's wrong with Indonesia's democratization? *Asian Journal of Social Science* 30(3): 547–569.

Trocki, C., ed. 1998. *Gangsters, democracy and the state in Southeast Asia.* Ithaca, NY: Cornell University Press.

van Klinken, G. 2001. The coming crisis in Indonesian area studies. *Journal of Southeast Asian Studies* 32(2): 263–268.

———. 2002. Indonesia's new ethnic elites. Indonesia in search of transition. H. Schulte Nordholt and I. Abdullah, eds., 65–105. Yogyakarta, Indonesia: Pustaka Pelajar.

Vanhanen, T. 1990. *The process of democratization: A comparative study of 147 states, 1980–1988.* New York: Crane Russak.

———. 1998. *Prospects for democracy in Asia*. London: Sterling Publishers.

Wanandi, J. 2002. Indonesia: A failed state? *The Washington Quarterly* 25(3): 135–146.

Weatherbee, D. 1985. Pancasila, politics and power. *Asian Survey* 25(2): 187–197.

———. 2002. Indonesia: Electoral politics in a newly emerging democracy. *How Asia votes.* J. Hseih and D. Newman, eds., 255–281. London: Chatham House.

Wessel, I., and G. Wimhofer, eds. 2001. *Violence in Indonesia*. Hamburg: Abera Publishing House.

Ying, D. 2001. Observations on Indonesia's electoral system, past and present. *Crafting Indonesian Democracy*. R. W. Liddle, ed., 119–125. Bandung: Indonesian Institute of Science.

Zenzie, C. 1999. Indonesia's new political spectrum. *Asian Survey* 39(2): 243–264.

Newspapers and News Periodicals

Aditjondro, G. 1998. Suharto and sons (and daughters, in-laws and cronies). *Washington Post*. Washington, July 10.

Aglionby, J. 2002. Indonesia takes a giant step down the road to democracy *The Guardian*. Manchester, August 11.

Aglionby, J. 2003a. Aceh peace provides ray of light. *The Guardian*. May 22.

Aglionby, J. 2003b. Ex-military chief charged with East Timor crimes. *The Guardian*. Manchester, February 26.

Aglionby, J. 2004. No peace of mind in Indonesia. *The Guardian*. Manchester, May 21.

Buchori, M. 2002. Two worldviews of Islam and the impacts. *Jakarta Post*. Jakarta, April 14: 11–12.

Colombijn, F. 1999. A peaceful road to freedom. *Inside Indonesia,* 60: 19.

Jakarta Post. 1999a. Will the students succeed? Jakarta, February 2.

———. 1999b. Political pacts have yet to include the people. Jakarta, November 23.

———. 2005. Political parties still lack maturity. Jakarta, May 12.

———. 2008a. Lawmaker, deputy governor arrested for graft. Jakarta, April 18.

———. 2008b. Opportunity there for KPK to take over BLBI probe. Jakarta, March 22.

Jones, S. 2002. Indonesia's war that won't go away. *The Guardian*. Manchester, August 4.

McCawley, T. 1999. Reforms aim to boost lending. *Asiaweek*. Hong Kong. March 20.

McCulloch, L. 2000. Business as usual. *Inside Indonesia*, Melbourne, July–September, **63**: 13–14.

Montagnon, P. 1999. In search of stability: The Indonesian general election on Monday will be a turning point in the country's efforts to establish itself as a democracy. *Financial Times*. London, June 4: 21–23.

Ramage, D. E. 2007. A reformed Indonesia. *Australian Financial Review*, Sydney, October 12.

Roosa, J. 2003. Brawling, bombing and backing: The security forces as a source of insecurity. *Inside Indonesia*, Melbourne, January–March, **73**: 10–11.

Sender, H. 1998. Smoke and mirrors. *Far Eastern Economic Review*, Hong Kong, **34**: 36.

Straits Times. 2004. PKS wins votes by downplaying Islamic agenda. Singapore, April 12.

Tesoro, J-M. 1999a. Insider outsider. *Asiaweek*, Hong Kong, December 31.

Tesoro, J-M. 1999b. Open but not shut. *Asiaweek*, Hong Kong, June 2.

Tornquist, O. 1999. The birth of world's third largest democracy. *Jakarta Post*. Jakarta, July 2–3.

Wanandi, J. 2006. Indonesian outlook. *Jakarta Post*. Jakarta, February 12.

Zarifi, S. 2004. A valid election in Aceh: Test case for Indonesia's democracy. *Jakarta Post*. Jakarta, July 3.

REPORTS AND SURVEYS

Cammack, D., D. McLeod, and A. Rocha Menocal. 2006. Donors and the "Fragile States" agenda: A survey of current thinking and practice. ODI Report submitted to the Japan International Co-operation Agency. London: Overseas Development Institute.

Human Rights Watch. 2001. Indonesia: The war in Aceh. *Human Rights Watch* **13**(4): 1–42.

———. 2003. Aceh under martial law: Inside the secret war. *Human Rights Watch* **15**(10): 1–50.

ICG. 2000. Indonesia: Keeping the military under control. ICG Asia Report No. 9., September 5. Jakarta/Brussels: International Crisis Group.

———. 2001. Aceh: Can autonomy stem the conflict? ICG Asia Report No. 18, June 27. Jakarta/Brussels: International Crisis Group.

———. 2002. Aceh: Slim chance for peace. ICG Indonesia Briefing, March 27. Jakarta/Brussels: International Crisis Group.

———. 2003a. Aceh: A fragile peace. ICG Asia Report No. 47, February 27. Jakarta/Brussels: International Crisis Group.

———. 2003b. Indonesia backgrounder: A guide to the 2004 elections. ICG Asia Report No. 71, December 18. Jakarta/Brussels: International Crisis Group.

———. 2005. Decentralisation and conflict in Indonesia: The Mamasa case. ICG Asia Briefing No. 37, May 3. Jakarta/Brussels: International Crisis Group.

IDEA 2000a. Democratization in Indonesia: An assessment. Stockholm: International Institute for Democracy and Electoral Assistance, Forum for Democratic Reform.

———. 2000b. Indonesia 2000: From *Reformasi* to democracy. Stockholm: International Institute for Democracy and Electoral Assistance, Forum for Democratic Reform.

———. 2005. One year after the elections: Is democracy in Indonesia on course? Stockholm: International Institute for Democracy and Electoral Assistance, Forum for Democratic Reform.

IHDR. 2004. The economics of democracy. Indonesia Human Development Report. Jakarta: United Nations Development Programme.

Jesudason, J. 2001. State legitimacy, minority political participation and ethnic conflict in Indonesia and Malaysia. *Social cohesion and conflict in Indonesia*, 65–98. Washington, DC: World Bank.

NDI. 1999. Indonesia's 7 June 1999 legislative elections—Tabulations of country votes. Post election statement No. 2, July 20. Washington, DC: National Democratic Institute.

UNDP. 2001. Human Development Report, 1–264. New York: United Nations Development Programme.

World Bank. 2004. Indonesia: Beyond macro-economic stability. Jakarta: World Bank.

INDEX